Punjabi Musalmans

J. M. Wikeley

Alpha Editions

This edition published in 2020

ISBN : 9789354040238

Design and Setting By
Alpha Editions
www.alphaedis.com
email - alphaedis@gmail.com

As per information held with us this book is in Public Domain. This book is a reproduction of an important historical work. Alpha Editions uses the best technology to reproduce historical work in the same manner it was first published to preserve its original nature. Any marks or number seen are left intentionally to preserve its true form.

PUNJABI MUSALMANS

Lt. Col. J.M. Wikeley

Second Edition

THE BOOK HOUSE
8, TRUST BUILDING P.O. BOX 734,
LAHORE.

Price Rs. 7-50

The aim in produciug this book is to put into an easily accessible form and as much informative as possible concerning the history, customs etc., of the people of Punjab who have embraced Islam. This book gives the origin and history of almost all the important Punjabi Tribes.

Publisher

CONTENTS

	Page
Chapter I : Punjabi Musalmans.	1
Chapter II : Sketch of the History of the Punjab.	13
Chapter III : History of Islam.	25
Chapter IV : Customs and Ceremonies of the Punjabi Musalmans.	47
Chapter V : Distribution of Tribes—Short Accounts of Punjabi Musalman Tribes.	65
Chapter VI : A Breif Account of Cis Indus Pathans and Tribes peculiar to Hazara District N. W. F. P and akin to Pathans.	151

PUNJABI MUSALMANS

Chapter I

The term Punjabi Musalmans roughly describes those Muslim Classes and Tribes which are to be found in that portion of the Punjab and North West Frontier Province which lies between the Indus and the Sutlej Rivers to the South of the main Himalayan Range. This includes Hazara District, portion of Jammu and Poonch (Kashmir territory), and the Hill Tracts of Rawalpindi District.

2. Four Main Divisions of Punjabi Musalmans.

Punjabi Musalmans may be classed under four main heads :—

(i) 1. Rajputs.

(ii) 2. Jats.

(iii) 3. Gujars.

(iv) 4. Others.

3. The history of the Punjab until the commencement of the Muhammadan invasions in A. D. 1001 is fragmentary and incomplete, interrupted by long periods of which we have no definite record. Certain incidents stand out as recorded facts and establish historical landmarks. Between these, nations, races and dynasties appear and disappear, leaving but faint traces of their existence to be unravelled by the Archaeological experts from their coins and inscriptions on stone and brass.

4. Origin of Punjabi Musalman Tribes.

Most Punjabi Musalman tribes trace their origin to

periods prior to the Muhammadan invasions, others claim fanciful or mythical ancestors, while the remainder are satisfied that they came into the country with the Muhammadan conquerors. The traditions of their past are, as a rule, handed down by the tribal 'mirasis' who record in song the exploits of their heroes. These bards keep the tribal genealogical tree, the roots of which extend back to some legendary hero : in some cases even to Adam.

In the absence of more satisfactory records we have generally to accept these statements, where they are not at variance with the opinion of ethnological authorities.

In chapter V there is a short account of each tribe, based on these sources of information. Only those tribes or sub-tribes are dealt with which are of some interest.

Below is the description of the four main divisions mentioned in paragraph 2.

RAJPUTS

Aryan Origin of Rajputs.

All 'Rajputs' claim Aryan origin and this claim has been accepted as correct by most ethnological authorities. Their common birth dates back, however, to so remote a past, that the term Rajput now describes races which are most dis-similar. The effects of time, claimate, and political vicissitudes have wrought great changes in the various branches of the race. We now find the Rajputs of Rajputhana differ greatly from the Rajputs of Southern Punjab and these again from the Rajputs of the North West portion of that province. In Punjab there are many types of the race, distinguished from one another by their moral and physical characteristics, and possessing, in varying degrees, the qualities which make good soldiers.

The Aryan descent of all Rajputs cannot be said to have been established beyond dispute, and it is probable that some, at least, of the Rajput tribes are of Scythian or Hun origin. It seems likely that most of the Punjabi Musalman Rajputs are sprung from this source, for they belong chiefly to the Agnicular or "Fire-born" tribes. "These are generally considered to have been Scythian warriors who assisted the Brahmans in their final struggle with the Buddhists, and were admitted into the ranks of the 'twice-born' as a reward for their services to Hinduism. The title 'Fire-born' was bestowed on them in order to distinguish them from the original Rajput races which claim descent from the Sun and Moon."

The word Rajputs is derived as follows :—

The Aryans having settled down in the lands they had won from the Dravidians, the aboriginal race, improved in civilization and by a process of natural selection gradually resolved themselves into three classes :—

(1) The *Barhman*, or priestly class.

(2) The *Kshatriya*, i.e., Rajput or governing and military caste, composed of the Maharajas and their warrior kinsmen and companions, whose duty it was to fight, rule and administer justice, and protect the community in general.

(3) The *Vaisiya*, or trading and agricultural caste, now represented by the Bunnia.

Rajput a Social Grade.

The *Rajput* therefore represented the aristocracy, and the word implies this distinction to this day. So much so is the case that Rajput in the Punjab has come to mean a social grade rather than an ethnological term.

The decennial censuses show how many tribes endeavour to substantiate their claim to high social position by returning themselves as 'Rajput', numbers of whom have no title to that distinction. Others have fallen to *Jat* status owing to their non-observance of those social laws recognised as necessary for the retention of their position as *Rajputs*. Many tribes have both a *Rajput* and a *Jat* branch, while others rank as Rajputs in one district and Jats in another.

So clearly is this social position of the *Rajput* recognised, that it is common to find men adding the word *Rajput* to the name of their tribe, even when the tribe is well known to have no claim whatever to *Rajput* origin ; it implies that the man considers himself to be of *Rajput* status.

Pride of Race or Tribe.

The Punjabi Musalman Rajput as a Rajput has what may be called a "pride of tribe' of which he is most tenacious and which he maintains by strict adherance to the rules which govern his marriage customs. He does not look on himself as a Rajput first and then as a *Gakhar*, or a *Janjua* or an *Awan*, but as member of one of these tribes first, and then as *Sahu* or as *Rajput* which entitles him to a certain social position. It is his tribe which distinguishes him and of which he is a proud member. This is a feeling which it is important to foster. He will not give his women in marriage to members of any tribe which is regarded as lower in the social scale than his own. As a rule he will not undertake menial labour, unless driven thereto by stress of circumstances. Those Punjabi Musalman tribes which have become lax in the observance of these social laws have inevitably fallen from the rank of Rajput to that of Jat.

The Aristocracy of the Rajput.

The Punjabi Musalman Rajputs belong to the aristocracy of the Punjab, and though a few other tribes consider themselves their equals, there are, with the exception of the *Sayads* and the *Gakhhars*, none that rank above them.

Conversion to Islam.

The general conversion of the Muslim Rajputs from Hinduism is supposed to have taken place towards the end of the 13th or early in the 14th century A. D. The Muslim conquests undoubtedly accelerated this change of religion, but the preaching of several renowned Muslim Saints, especially Bawa Farid of Pakpattan and Syed Ali Hijveri (Data Gunj Bakhsh) of Lahore, whose eloquence drew large numbers to hear them, helped considerably to this end.

Separation of the Hindu Rajput from the Musalman Rajput.

Prior to the Muslim conquests the whole of the Punjab and Northern India was ruled by the Rajput princes. The decissive battles of Thanesur, Kanouj and Benares fought by Muhammad Ghori in 1193 A. D.

against the Rajputs and Rathors, broke up their power and their effective combination. A great immigration of Rajputs into Marwar and Northern and Western Rajputana then followed, and in that quarter they became the ruling race ; there they retained their independence and religion, and the final separation between the two branches (Hindu and Muslim) was then complete.

Military service is looked on by the best Punjabi Muslim Rajputs in their true 'Metier', and all the best known families have given their sons to the Army.

JATS

Origin.

The origin of the people known as Jats in the North Western Punjab, and as *Jats* East and South of the Sutlej, has been the subject of much learned discussion by ethnological authorities, and very divergent views have been expressed. No degree of certainty has been reached, and what the *Jats* are, or whence they came, is still an historical problem which remains to elucidated by archeaological or other antiquarian research.

Conjectures as to Origin of Jats.

The *Jats* have been identified by one writer with the gypsies of Europe, another makes their original home in the Mesopotamian marshes, others again consider them to be the descendants of the *Jatii*, *Getae* and other Scythian races, which entered India about the beginning of the Christian era. Recent opinion, however, leads to the conjecture that at no time has there been a *Jat* or *Jaat* race as distinct from the Rajput race. It is probable that both have spung from the same Ayran stock.

"Jat" Signifies Social Status.

Whatever the origin of the term Jat may be, it now signifies in the North Western Punjab an occupation or degree of social status, rather than a tribe or race. *Rajputs* represent the highest social grade while *Jats* may be considered to rank next to them.

The term *Jat* is also used to describe an occupation: in one locality it means the cultivator or "Jat Zamindar", in another it is applied to the camel-driver, and elsewhere to cattle graziers. Jats are essentially tillers of the soil and as cultivators they superior to Rajputs.

Jat Claim to Rajput Descent.

In fact, most Jat tribes trace their origin from Rajput status, and ascribe their fall in social rank to the mesalliance of some Rajput prince or princess with a person of lower grade. To lay down a common ancestry for all Punjabi Musalman Jats and to describe them as distinctive race, is warranted by neither historical facts, tribal legends, nor distinctive physiognomy. The majority of the traditions of the Jat tribes in the Punjab point to their being recent arrivals in the land of their adoption.

Stability for the Army.

From a recruiting point of view *Jats* vary considerably according to the locality in which they are found. While in one district they are not good, in another they are well worthy of consideration. The Muslim Jats of the Eastern Punjab and the districts bordering on it, are a very different people to the Jats of the North West, and these again from the Jats of Multan.

Jats often to be Prefered to Rajputs.

There are Jat tribes which in every way, physique, spirit and manliness, are to be prefered as soldiers to others of Rajput status.

Mention of Jats in History.

Subsequent to the first Muhammadan invasions we find the Jats frequently mentioned in history. In 1024 A. D. Mahmud of Ghazni had great difficulty in overcoming the *Jats of Sind*, and he is said to have finally reduced them after a naval engagement near Multan, presumably on the Chenab. It is probable, however, that the word *Jat* has been used in a very loose sense by the historians who relates this event. In 1658 A. D. the Jats appear as valuable allies to Aurangzeb in the troubled times that followed the deposition of Shah Jehan. Babar mentions the *Jats* of the Salt Range in his memoirs.

Good Physique of Jats.

In the area where water is scarce, the Jats are a pastoral people owning in one place cattle, in another camels. The opening of the great Punjab canals has effected them greatly and now they are well-to-do cultivators. Their occupations, especially in localities where they have led a pastoral life, have affected their physique favourably; they are, as a rule, heavy thickest men with good chests. Their mental equipment is also now appreciable due to their paying attention to Education.

Conversion to Islam.

It is uncertain when the Jats and Gujars of the Punjab embraced Islam, but when Baber invaded India in

1525 A. D. he found that in the Salt Range they had been subdued by the Awans, Janjuas and other Rajput tribes, which had adopted the Muslim religion; we may conclude therefore that they were Muslims. Punjabi Musalman *Jats* have been, and still are, democratic in their tribal arrangements.

PUNJABI MUSALMAN GUJARS

Origin.

While the *Jatii* and *Getae* were moving into India from the Kandahar valley, another Scythian tribe called the *Yuch-Chi*, whose modern representatives are the *Gujars*, had established themselves in Kabul, Kashmir and the Northern Punjab, where their settlements may be traced in the names of places and districts such as Gujranwala and Gujrat. Before the end of the 3rd century a portion of *Yuch-Chi* had begun to move Southward and were shortly afterwards separated from their Northern brethren by the advance of the *Getae* or *Jats* from the Bolan.

As has before been noticed, the distinction between Jats, Gujars and Rajputs is probably social rather than ethnic. Those families of the Aryo-Scythian stock whom the tide of fortune raised to political importance, became Rajputs, almost by virtue of their rise, and their descendants have retained the title with the privileges by observing the rules by which the higher are distinguished from the lower castes in Hindu scale of precedence ; by refusing to intermarry with families of inferior rank ; by rigidly abstaining from widow-marriage ; and by refraining from menial and degrading occupations. Those who transgressed these rules fell from their high estate and were reduced, some to the grade of *Jats* or cultivators, others to that of *Gujar* or *herdsman*.

Gurjara Empire.

Indian history also mentions an obscure tribe known as the *Gurjaras* who apparently flourished in the North West for the short period about the 3rd or 4th century A. D. One authority fixes as Gurjara Empire, with its capital at Kanauj and embracing nearly the whole of Northern India, about A. D. 840 under Bhojal. This tribe is supposed to be of Scythian or Hun origin. It seems more than probable that the words *Gujar*, *Gujrat* and *Gujarat* are derived from this source. But the origin in history of the Gujaras is so obscure that no definite statement can be made on the subject.

Gujars, a Pastoral People.

The Gujars as a race have always been recognised as a pastoral people, and the larger portion of them occupy themselves with the herding of cattle, sheep and goats. They are found throughout the Punjab; in some localities they belong to the resident population and combine cultivation of land with the herding of cattle, in others they are purely nomadic. As already mentioned the Punjabi Musalman Gujars were probably converted to the Muslim faith during the 15th Century A. D. The Punjabi Musalman Gujar is a patient tiller of the soil, and his physique is good. As in the case of Punjabi Musalman Jats it is impossible to describe the characteristics of all Punjabi Musalman Gujars as being alike. Both vary with the locality in which we find them, and the ocupation which they follow. The education standard of this tribe is now raising.

OTHER TRIBES

Among Punjabi Musalmans there are certain tribes

which claim to be of other origin than that of Rajput, Jat or Gujar. Those may be classed as Foreign tribes as there advent into India is of comparatively recent date. They came with the Muslim conquerers and have always been Musalmans by religion.

Arab Invasion of Sind.

The Arabs were the first Muslim conquerers of India; they appeared in Sind during 8th century A D. having landed at a point near the site of Modern Karachi. They overcame the Brahmans and, leaving a garrison behind, marched up the Right bank of Indus. Defeating Brahman armies *en route* they finally captured Multan.

No Punjabi Musalman tribes appear to claim descent from these Arabs, though it may be that with these adventures came the first *Sayads* and *Koreshis*.

Awans and Gakkhars.

Mahmud of Gazni was the next Muslim Conquerer of India (1001 A. D.). Several tribes, notably the Gakkhars and Awans claim to have come with him, through it is difficult to reconcile their statements with historical records of the time.

Turks and Mughuls.

Both Timur and Babar brought *Turks* and *Mughals* with them. From the latter a number of tribes claim to be descended, and it is now the fashion for many Punjabi Musalman tribes to call themselves Mughals. Among these are the Khattars, Kassars, Ghebas and others. Of the *Turks* but few remain, a single tribe in Hazara being the sole representative.

Persians.

The Gakkhars are the only tribe which claims

Persian origin. If we except Darius who sent an expedition to India about 500 B. C., the only Persian monarch who invaded India was Nadir Shah in 1739 A. D. He came and went, but leaving no garrison and no Persian rule.

Sayads, Koreshis and Sheikhs.

The Sayads and Koreshis are Arabs, the former being the direct descendants of the Prophet's tribe, the ancient guardian of the "Kaaba" at Mecca. Both tribes have many branches, which claim to have come into India at different periods.

Shiekhs.

The only caste which includes miscellaneous converts is the "Sheikh", which is really a title of respect and was applied originally to the Arab spirtual guides.

These tribes have little to distinguish them from the ordinary Punjabi Musalman Rajput ; except in rare instances (especially among true Moghals) their physiognomy and characteristics are those of the people among whom they lies.

A further account of them will be found in Chapter V.

Pathans.

Inhabiting Hazara District, North West Frontier Province, and the banks of the Indus in Attock and Mianwali Districts are purely Pathan tribes and tribes allied to Pathans.

These tribes are fully dealt with in Chapter VI.

Chapter II

SKETCH OF THE HISTORY OF THE PUNJAB

The history of the Punjab before the advent of the Muslims, is a record of legendary events, obscure dynasties and foreign invasions, the sequence of which has not yet to be clearly established.

It is difficult to fix definitely when legend ends and true history begins.

The first event which stands out as a solid historical fact, recorded by trustworthy writers, is the campaign of Alexander the Great, in B. C. 327-324.

Before this (with the exception of the Persian expedition under Syklax), we have to rely for our knowledge on the legends contained in the Vedas; after it, the scanty information we possess has been obtained from the coins and inscriptions found in various parts of the country, and, for short periods, from the memoirs of two Chinese writers.

The record of the expedition under Syklax was found in Persia, and is contained in two inscriptions. The force was sent out by Darius 1 of Persia between 521 and 484 B. S. It passed through the Punjab and Syklax "Fitting out a Fleet of boats, navigated the Indus to its mouth and utlimately returned home by a sea route". (Thompson).

He thus anticipated Alexander's similar movement by over 160 years. A portion of the Punjab is supposed to have formed a Satrapy of the Persian Empire of Darius, and later it may have been included in the Achaemenian Empire of that country.

Many centuries before this the Aryans are supposed to have entered India from the North West. They came in succeeding hordes which followed each other at great intervals of time.

Until recently the approximate date of those immigrations was fixed at between 2,000 and 1,000 B. C., but Pandit Hari Kishan Kaul, in his "Report on the Census of 1911", has antedated the Aryan invasion by 3,000 years, and fixes the date of the first Aryan movement as being not later than 5 000 B. C. This learned writer's conclusions are based on Count Bjournstjerna's "Theogany of the Hindus", and are further strengthened by certain dates, fixed astrologically, in the Vedas.

"That ancient Bactrian documents called the "Dabistan" found in Kashmir by Sir W. Jones gives a list of Bactrian kings, who were Hindus whose first king reigned in Bactria, 5,000 years before Alexander's expedition to India. And what would thus prove that India was linked with Bactria, and enjoyed a splendid civilization 6,000 B. C./or nearly 8,000 years ago."

We know very little of the Aryans, and all we do know has gathered from the ancient Hindu documents, the Rig Veda.

We learn that the Aryans overcame the aboriginal tribes, whom they drove before them as they penetrated into the country.

These aborigines have been named *Dravidians* :

nothing is, however, known about them, and their origin is hid in the mists of antiquity. The wild and semi-wild tribes of India, such as *Sonthals* and the *Bhils* and others, are supposed to be their descendants.

It is probable that a large portion of the *Dravidians* became subjects of Aryans, and an inter-mixture of blood may have taken place.

Each successive swarm of the Aryans pushed their predecessors further into India, East and South.

The Aryans founded the Hindu religion and divided themselves into three great branches or castes:—

The *Brahmans*—the *Kushtriyas*—and the *Vaisiyas*, which represented the Priestly caste, the Ruling or Fighting caste and the Trading or working caste.

The country was divided into principalities, under different rulers who waged war on one another.

Hinduism was the religion of the country, and the *Brahmans* paramount, until the 4th Century B. C. when a change came. *Gautama*, the Buddha, commenced his teaching, Budhism increased rapidly, rose to its zenith under Asoka—272-231 B. C.—and remained the popular religion for over 600 years.

In 327 B. C. Alexander the Great appeared on the scene. His Army entered India in two columns, the first followed the Kabul river into the Peshawar valley and established itself on the right bank of the Indus near Attock, where a bridge to span the river was commenced.

Alexander led the second column through the mountainous country north of the Peshawar velly and the *Yusufzai* plains: the brave tribes of these hills were overcome and the flank of the great Army made secure. Crossing the Indus, Alexander entered the kingdom of Ambhi, who reigned over the territories lying between that river and the Jhelum, and who had already tendered his submission. The Macedonians were guests rather than conquerers while at Taxila, the capital of Ambhi's kingdom. Taxila has been indentified with the ruin mounds near Shah-ki-Dheri in the Rawalpindi district, and extensive excavations are now in progress on the former site of this city, under the direction of the Archaeological department.

A very complete account of Taxila, its institutions, religion and learning has been recorded by Aryan, the historian of Alexander's campaign. The brilliant exploits which followed and their termination in the death of Alexander while in Persia, are too well known to need further record here.

The effects of the campaign were but transitory, and the history of the Punjab was unaffected by them. The *Brahmanical* chronicles do not even mention Alexander's name, though his fame is established throughout Muslim Asia.

The Macedonian garrisons were driven out of the country or submerged by 324 B. C.

All the time of Alexander's visit the Punjab appears to have been under the rule of three kings, the names— Ambhi, Porus and Mousikanos have come down to us. The *Mouryas* dynasty, which consolidated these territories under one throne, and which ruled the Punjab (as well as a great portion of India), came in with Chandra Gupta in 321 B. C. and lasted for about 90 years. The great Budhhist king Asoka, belonged to this line, and has left lasting monuments of his piety in the edicts, named after him, and found throughout India.

Then followed the *Bactrians*, *Parthias*, and *Kushan* dynasties, which bring us into the third century of our era.

The Bactrians had attained a considerable degree of Greek civilization, and their ruling classes were Macedonian and Greek. Their princes appear to have ruled the Punjab from the fall of the Mauryan dynasty until about the end of the second century B. C., when the Parthians came on the scene.

The *Parthians* came from the country to the South-east of the Caspian Sea, and are described as a nation of fierce horsemen. They were followed in the first century A. D. by the *Kushan* emperors, who belonged to that section of a people known as the *Yuch-chi*.

The best known of these emperors was Kanishka, whose empire included Bactria, Afghanistan, Kashmir and Eastern Turkistan as well as the Punjab. Kanishka, like Asoka, encourged Buddhism, and his name as celebrated in China and Tibet as that of Ashoka in Burma and Ceylon. His capital was at Peshawar, then known as Purushapura. 2nd Century A. D. has been fixed as being the period in which this monarch reigned.

During the 3rd and 4th centuries A. D. the history of the Punjab is shrouded in obscurity. The Gupta dynasty, commencing with a second Chandra Gupta, appeared in the south, about 320 A. D., but the Punjab does not seem to have come under its sway.

" The White Huns entered the Punjab early in the 6th century and remained in power until about the year 530 A. D. Their capital was Sakala, now identified with Sialkot, and their best known kings were Toramana and Mihiragula, of whom the latter overran Kashmir.

These *Huns* "were akin to those other *Huns*, who ravaged the east of Europe and spread their terror far and wide by the savagery of their manners and the uncouthness of their appearance. They were a race of the Mongolian type with the high cheek bones, sunken eyes and snub noses." (Thompson's History of India). With them were associated, in some obscure manner, a people known as the Gurjara.

Though the power of the Huns did not last long, they left their mark on the history, "And added a new element to the population of India". (Thompson). One of the Royal clans of Rajputana— the Hunas, may possibly be their descendants, and a small Rajput tribe in the Punjab is known as Hun.

The Gurjara are supposed by some to be the ancestors of the Gujars and have left their name in—Gujar Khan, Gujrat, Gujranwala and Gujarat. The downfall of the Huns was accomplished by the Yasodharman, whose name only has come down to us. A gap of about 100 years follows this obscure event. This period Budhhism lost its place as the popular religion of the country, and the Brahmans again raised Hinduism in its former position and themselves to power. This change was not brought about by peaceful methods alone, and the *Agnicular* or "Fire-born" *Rajputs* tribes are said to have owed their admission into the fold for the help they gave to the Brahmans during their struggle for supermacy.

After the Huns—630 A. D.—The Punjab appears to have come under the rule of petty Rajput princes, who parcelled out the country into small independent states, of which, early in the 8th century, the most important had their capital at Garh Gajni (Rawalpindi), Sialkot, and Lahore. The Hindu kings of Kashmir probably ruled a part of it until the end of the 9th century, when the North West Punjab west of the river Jhelum, came under the Brahman rulers of Kabul, known as Shahi kings. It was these kings whom Sabuttagin, the first of the Ghaznawid (Muslim) dynasty overcame.

In 712 A. D. Islam made its first appearance in the country with Arab conquerors of Sindh.

The Arabs under Muhammad Bin Kasim, a cousin of the Governer of the province Babylonia, under the country near modern Karachi. A portion of their force came overland while the remainder were conveyed by an Arab fleet. Overcoming the Hindu Kings they marched up the right bank of the Indus, and finally established themselves at Multan. "The Arab soldiers remained in Sindh, where they formed Military colonies and settled down in permanent occupancy. When the powers of the Khalif of Baghdad and of the Provincial Governor declined, the local rulers became independent. From about the year 879 A. D. there were Sultans reigning at Mansura and Multan." (Thompson's History of India) Their power did not however, last long, and their advent made little or no change in the religion of the country.

Sabuktagin, the first of the Ghaznawids, added **Kabul** and Peshawar, to his dominions, and defeated Jaipal, King of Lahore, at Lamghan in 988 A. D. He was succeeded by his son, Mahmud of Ghazni, in 988 A.D., and followed the Muslim conquerors of India. Mahmud is said to have undertaken 17 campaigns against India. Mahmud's first great battle was against Jaipal, who had suffered defeat at the hands of his father in 988 A. D. The fight is believed to have taken place on the Chach plain near Hazro on the Indus. The *Gakkhars*, at that time a very powerful race, who held all the hilly country from the Margalla pass to the Jhelum, made an impetuous change with 30,000 men on Mahmud's camp and almost decided the fate of the day in favour of Jaipal, but Mahmud averted disaster and won the battle. In the year 1009 A. D. Mahmud met the *Rajput* confederacy under Anandpal, the son of Jaipal, at Bhatinda, and for the second time the *Gakkhars* were nearly succeeding in turning the scale in favour of Rajputs when. Anandpal's elephant, which had been wounded, bolted from the field, and the Hindus concluding that their leader was fleeing, gave away. Mahmud thus won his second great victory.

Mahmud was succeeded by his son Muhammad, who was early deposed by Masud, another son, and put to death in 1030 A. D. Masud emulated his father with but poor success. and lost most of the territory he had won: Ghazni and a portion of the Punjab alone remained.

The Ghaznawids were expelled from Ghazni in 1155 **A.D.** by Ala-ud-din Ghori, and the last of them took refuge in Lahore where he was captured by Muhammad Ghori in 1185 A. D.

Muhammad Ghori, also known as Shahab-ud-din

Ghori, was a nephew of Ala-ud-din, the Ghori chief, from the mountains to the west of Ghazni. Mahmud of Ghazni has been able to keep these chiefs in check, but on the decline of the Ghaznawids they rose in power and finally, as we have seen, wrested Ghazni and the Punjab from the house of Ghazni.

The *Rajput* Chiefs formed a coalition under Prithviraj to stem the torrent of Muslim invasion, and Muslim met Hindu near Karnal in 1191 A. D. Muhammad Ghori was defeated and his army fled. The following year, however, Muhammad Ghori again led an army against the *Rajputs*, a battle was fought on the same ground as in the previous year, and this time Muslims were victorious. Delhi was captured and became the c e n t r e of Muhammadan power.

Muhammad Shahab-ud-din Ghori was assassinated in 1206 A. D. by a hand of *Gakkhar* or *Khokhar* (it is uncertain which) who swam the river Indus and entered his tent at night.

The *Ghoris* were followed by the dynasty known as the Slave Kings, which commenced with Aibak, and ruled at Delhi from 1206 to 1290 A. D. It was during the reign of Altamash of this line that the Moghals first appeared : Chingiz Khan ravaged the Punjab and Sindh.

After the Slave Kings came the Afghans known as Khaljis 1290-1320 A. D. who were followed by the Tuglak Shahis, 1320-1412 A. D.

The Punjab, to the west of the Sutlej, appears at this time to have been under the rule of governors appointed from Dehli.

Taimur the Tartar (a Moghal) entered India in 1398 A. D. He crossed the Indus at Attock and marched on Delhi, meeting with no opposition on the way. Delhi was taken after a battle fought under its walls. Taimur remained in Delhi only a fortnight, and during his return waged a war against the Hindus of the Himalayan valleys.

From 1412 to 1526 A. D. there was no permanant power ruling in India, and the Punjab appears to have been held by Viceroys, nominally under the authority of the king of Delhi, but in reality more or less independent.

In 1414 A. D. the *Sayad*, Khizr Khan, Governor of Multan, siezed the throne and established a line known as the *Sayads*, who were followed by the *Lodhis*, and Afghan clan, from 1451 to 1526 A. D. The third king of this dynasty gave great offence to the Afghan nobles, and one of them who was then Governor of the Punjab "Invited the Moghul Babar, to step in and redress their grievances" (Thompson).

Babar, sixth in descent from Taimur, advanced on Delhi, and at Panipat, in April 1526 A. D. fought one of the decissive battles of the world and gained a great victory. He elected to stay in the country : and with him commenced the line of the great Moghal Emperors.

Until the decline of the Moghal power in 1707 A. D. the Punjab was under the form of a settled Government, and in Akbar's reign formed one of the fifteen "Subahs" or provinces, under a Viceroy.

The year 1739 A. D. is memorable for the invasion of Nadir Shah. That such an expedition was possible shows the state of decay and weakness to which the Moghal power had fallen. Another battle was fought near Karnal, and Delhi was sacked for the third time. Nadir Shah took away with him to Parsia an immense amount of booty, which included the famous Peacock throne and the *Koh-i-nur*.

During this period, with the loss of all central control from Delhi, the Punjab seems to have broken away from authority and to have formed a system of small states owned by petty tribes, which were more or less independent. There were the *Gakkhars* in the hill country between the Margalla pass and the Jhelum, the *Janjuas* and *Awans* in the Salt Range, the *Sials* of Jhang, the Kharrals of Montgomery, and others, who appointed their own chiefs and formed their own revenues. Matters remained in this state until the *Sikhs* rose to power and asserted their authority from Lahore. *Sikh Sardars* were placed as Governors and, backed up by *Sikh* troops, took over the revenue.

This was not accomplished without severe fighting, and some of the tribes, notably the *Gakkhars* and *Janjuas* gave the *Sikhs* infinite trouble.

From the latter half of the 18th century the North West Punjab was under *Sikh* dominion, and it so remained until the country was taken over by the British after the second *Sikh* war in 1849.

This short sketch of the history of the Punjab shows that, from earliest times, the movement of the peoples into the Punjab has been from the North West. Until comparatively recent times almost each century has been the arrival of new races—**Aryans, Bactrians, Scythians, Huns** and many others, differing widely in race, in culture and physiognomy, have entered the Punjab : some have remained and some passed on further east and south. It is impossible that there has been no intermingling of blood and it becomes exceedingly difficult to fix, with any degree of accuracy, the origin of most of the tribes which we now call *Punjabi Musalmans*.

There has, however, been also another current of immigration into the Punjab which this account cannot show, viz from Rajputana and Hindustan into the southern and eastern parts of the Punjab, and is isolated instances, even further north.

The details of this second movement are most obscure and its causes not easily explained. The *Manj, Punwar* and *Chauhan Rajputs* appear to have been those which were most effected by it. The best known of these movements occured in the reign of Ala-ud-din, of the Khalji dynasty (1296-1316), when the ancestors of the *Kharrals, Tiwanas, Ghebas* and *Chaddars*, emigrated from the Provinces of Hindustan to the Punjab.

Some retained their status and name of *Rajput* while others became Jats, but the tribes which have resulted from this second movement are probably of purer Rajput and Jat descent than the other Punjabi Musalmans who claim the same origin.

Though Punjabi Musalmans have been devided into four main sections, Rajputs Jats Gujars and other tribes, in another chapter, it must not be concluded that this division is ethnologically correct.

Chapter III

HISTORY OF ISLAM

Birth of Muhammad (Be Peace upon him)

Muhammad (Be peace upon him), the founder of the Musalman religion, was born at Mecca in the year 570 A. D. His parents belonged to the *Koresh* tribe. The sanctity of the *Koresh* dates from nearly two centuries before the birth of Muhammad (Be peace upon him), at which period the tribe acquired the guardianship of the "Kaaba" at Mecca. The "Kaaba" is said to have been built by prophet Abraham, and from remote antiquity, had been a centre of pilgrimage and worship for all the tribes of Arabia.

The Arabs at this time were steeped in Idolatry and their religion was decrepit and effete. Muhammad (Be peace upon him) received light from heavens and declared that he is a prophet, commissioned by the only GOD, to put down the idolatry, and restore the religion of Abraham. He told about the Day of Judgment when everyone will appear before the Creator of the World and will be rewarded for his *goods* and punished for his *sins*. The Meccans were annoyed with this announcement, for the Gods denounced by Muhammad (Be peace upon him) were their holy things and their attachment to the traditional worship of their fathers was the greater since the prosperity of their town rested upon the sanctity of the "Kaaba," which, besides being a great centre of pilgrimage, was also a trading mart for all the tribes of Arabia.

During the next few years Muhammad (be peace upon him) endured every species of insult and persecution, at the hands of the people of Mecca. He finally decided to abandon Mecca and fled to Yathreb, whose inhabitants had taken kindly to the new doctrine. This flight or "Hijra" took place in 622 A. D. and has become the era of Islam. It marks the establishment of a new religion destined to be one of the most powerful influences of civilization the world has ever known. Yathreb was henceforth named the city of the Prophet "Madinat-un-Nabi" or shortly Madina. Muhammad (be peace upon him) was elected chief magistrate of Madina. By wise decisions and the creation of law and justice where previously only violence existed, the people of Madina became his great lovers and devotees.

After a series of victories which he was granted from Almighty, he advanced to Mecca where he entered as a victorious. While entering in Mecca, Muhammad (be peace upon him) declared that there should be no bloodshed. He took pains to preserve the sanctity of the city, and confirmed all its rights and privileges. Besides the abolishing of idols, every sanctuary, execpt the "Kaaba," was destroyed. "Kaaba" was declared the recognised centre of Islam.

After that, the faith of Islam rapidly spread throughout Arabia. In 632 A D. at the time of the death of Muhammad (Be peace upon him) the Arabia was full of true Muslims. Within six years of his death Islam speard over Syria, Persia and Egypt, which was in fact due to the sincere efforts of the true believers of the Prophet. Islam was meant to throw light of civilization on the whole world and this light was spread over a great part of the world by the followers of Muhammad (Be peace upon him) who understood the reality and importance of Islam. Rome, Africa and Spain were introduced with the Islamic civilization, and within a century the true Muslims had pushed their conquests into the heart of France. All Europe would probably have been overrun by the soldiers of the Crescent, had not the Muslims stopped their advancement.

On the death of Muhammad (be peace upon him) Hazrat Abu Bakr was appointed "Khalifa" the Amir-ul-Musalmeen. Hazrat Abu Bakr died in 634 A. D. and was succeeded by Hazrat Omar the Great. Hazrat Omar the Great died in 644 A. D. and was succeeded by Hazrat Osman. Hazrat Osman faced amutiny in 656 A. D. in which he lost his life. On Hazrat Osman's assassination Hazrat Ali was elected *Khalif* unconditionally. He, however, met with much opposition from Moawiyeh, a follower of his predecessor, who compelled him to come to terms. This led to a conspiracy among his own partisans, three of whom murdered him at the doors of a mosque. A great mausoleum was afterwards erected over his tomb, which became the site of the town of Meshed, one of the holiest shrines of the Shiah pilgrims.

On Hazrat Ali's death in 661 A.D. his eldest son Imam Hassan was elected to the Khalifate, but he resigned office in favour of Moawiyeh, on condition that he should resume it on the latter's demise. Moawiyeh, however, who wished his son Yazid to succeed him, caused Hassan to be murdered by his wife. Yazid succeeded his father, and the Omayyad dynasty was thus firmly established in the Khalifate.

Up to this time the office of *Khalifa* was elective and

democratic, but Moawiyeh, whilst retaining the form of election, made it in reality hereditary.

With the accession of Moawiyeh the Omayyad came into power, and from this time, the feud between the Hashmi (the Koresh tribe to which Muhammad (be peace upon him) belonged and the Omayyad, which originated two centuries before the birth of the Prophet (be peace upon him) and had been passed on from generation to generation, received fresh impulse.

Imam Hussain, the second son of Khalifa Ali, has never acknowledged the title of Yazid, and when the Muslims of Mesopotamia invited him to release them from the Omayyad, he proceeded to Iraq, accompanied by his family and a few retainers, to place himself at the head of the former. On the way, at Kerbala, Imam Hussain was overtaken by an Omayyad army and, after a heroic struggle lasting four days, he and his following were all slaughtered, save the women and a child named Ali.

This took place on the 10th of *Muharram* in the year 680 A. D. It is in Commemoration of this event that the *Shiahs* of Pakistan, India and Persia observe the first ten days of the *Muharram* as a period of mourning.

Thus within Islam, from earliest times, there have been two faction, the Hashmites and the Omayyad. The Hashmites are to-day, generally represented by the *Shiahs*, and the Omayyad by the *Sunnis*.

The *Shiahs* believe in the absolute sanctity of the Descendants of Hazrat Ali. They maintain that on the death of Prophet Muhammad (be peace upon him) the office of Khalif is vested by divine right in Hazrat Ali, and after him in his two sons Imam Hassan and Imam Hussain, and they reject as usurpers, the first three Khalifs.

They detest the memory of the Omayyad Khalifs who wrested the Khalifate from its rightful holder and in particular, that the Yazid, who slew the martyr Imam Hussain. They observe the first ten days of Muharram as a fast in commemoration of the martyrdom of Hazrat Ali and his sons, and carry about "*Taziahs*," meant to represent the tombs of the two latter, with loud lamentation and mourning.

The *Sunnis* observe only the tenth day of Muharram and abhor the "taziahs". They consider themselves the only true followers of Muhammad (be peace upon him) on the ground that they accepted Hazrat Abu Bakr, Hazrat Omar the Great and Hazrat Osman as rightful *Khalifs* and that they submit themselves the authority of the "Sunneh" or "Hadis," recognising six books of "Hadis." *Shiahs* recognise only four books.

The religion of Islam.

The *Sunnis* are devided into four schools—*Hanafi*, *Shafi*, *Maliki* and Hambali. Majority belong to the first.

The *Shiah* or Imamate doctrine indicates the Imamate being a light (nur) which passed by natural descent from one to the other, the Imam are divine, and this heritage is inalienable. Thus the second Imam, Hassan, the eldest son of Hazrat Ali, although he resigned the Khalifate could not resign the Imamate which had descended to him, and on his death passed by inheritance to Imam Hussain. Its subsequent devolution followed the natural line of descent, thus :—

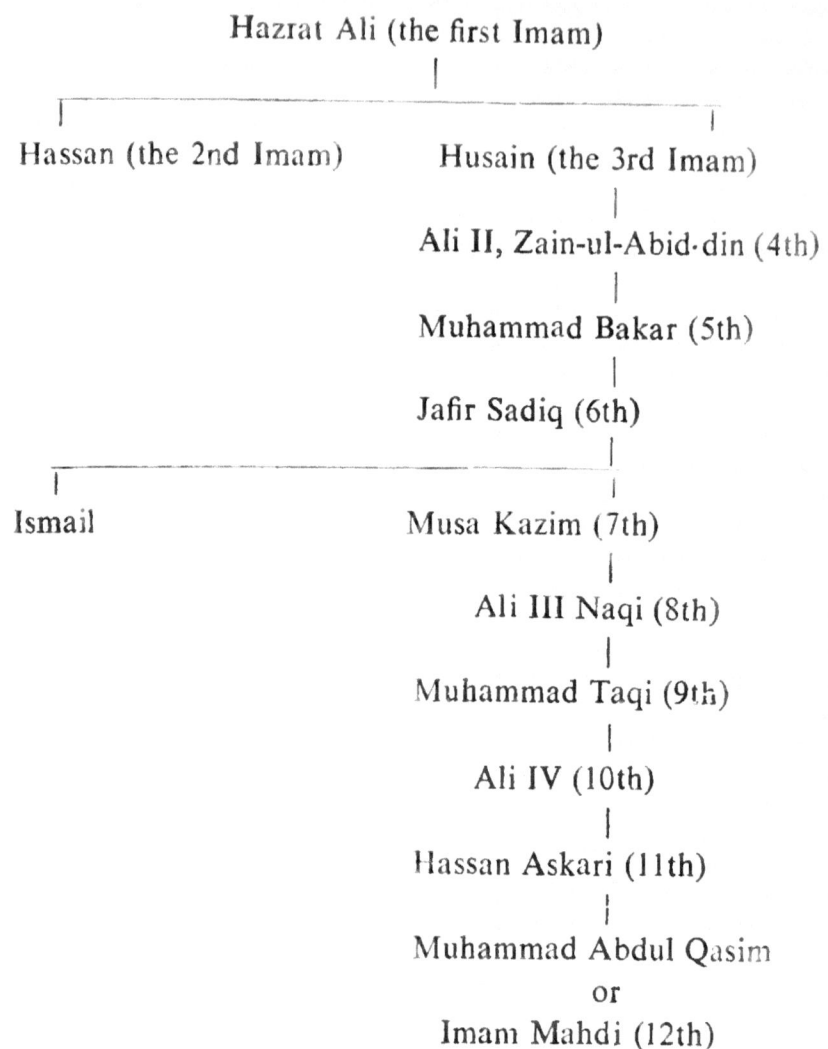

Jafir, the sixth Imam, nominated Ismail, his eldest son, but on the latter's premature death he declared that Musa was his heir to the exclusion of Ismail's children.

The claims of Ismail were supported by one party among the *Shiah* despite the declaration of Jafir, and thus was founded the *Ismail* sect who held that the last visible Imam was Ismail, after whom commenced the succession of concealed Imams.

The other party, the Imamites, support the claims of Musa, and believes that the 12th Imam, Muhammad Abdul Qasim, is still alive that he wanders over the earth and is destined to re-appear.

Shiahs and Sunnis have minor differences is their manner of offering prayers and performing ablution. The principal difference being that Sunnis, when praying, cross the arms over the breast, while Shiahs, keep the arms straight by the sides.

Another sect which may be mentioned is that of the *Wahabis*, founded by Muhammad Ibn Abdul Wahab. This sect are very puritanical and rejected all traditional teaching except that of the Prophet's (be peace upon him) companions. They prohibit pilgrimages to shrines or tombs, and in other respects try to restore Islam to its pristine purity. They are extremely fond of advocating 'Jihad' or Holy wars against infidels.

The great majority of Punjabi Musalmans are *Sunnis*.

DOCTRINE

The *Koran* is the Holy book of Islam, embodying the orders of Almighty and the teaching and precepts of the Prophet (be peace upon him) The work is written in prose, and apart from its religious importance, is a model of literary elegance, and a perfect storehouse of the purest and most classical Arabic. The name given to this religion is Islam, signifying 'safety' or 'salvation' its adherents being called either Musalmans, Muslims, or Momins.

The cardinal principle of Islam is a belief in the Unity of God and the acceptance of Muhammad (be peace upon him) as the messenger of God. "The central porposition which regulates the structure of Islam, is that there is fear in Nature, and the object of Islam is to free man from fear. It is fear that dominates man. The essential nature of man consists in will, not intellect or understanding. That a man's fate is written on his forehead is entirely of Hindu origin." (Extract from a lecture by Dr. Sh. Muhammad Iqbal).

The *Koran* inculcates belief in the immortality of the soul, man's moral resposibility for his life on earth, a day of judgment, and in the hereafter a reward of existence in paraside, or a punishment.

The Muslim creed enjoins prayer, charity, truthfulness industry and thrift, justice, devotion and humanity to animals.

Periodical fasting as an excercise in subjugation of the senses, and purification before prayer are prescribed. As regards the former "but he amongst you who shall be ailing or on a journey (shall fast) an equal number of other days, and they that are able to keep it (and do not) shall make atonement by maintaining a poor man". Regarding the latter, purification, the hands, face and feet as the parts most likely to be soiled, is intended. Conditions may exist, however, which may render ablutions impossible and a soldier in the field, a traveller in the desert, the denizens of a wintry land, and others similarly situated, may dispense with ablution before prayer.

Hajj.

To keep alive the feeling of brotherhood and to perpetuate the memory of the sacred spot where the great message was delivered, Muslims are directed if circumstances permit, to make a pilgrimage to Mecca (The Hajj).

A man may marry one, two, three or four wives provided he can deal with them "equity." Divorce is allowed.

Envy and mischief-making, pride and vanity, are alike condemned, and compulsion in religion is strictly forbidden. Drinking intoxicants is reprehended.

RELIGIOUS OBSERVANCES AND FESTIVALS

The Khutbah.

The khutbah is the oration or sermon delivered every Friday and on the Idul Fitr and the Id-ul-Zuha, after the mid-day prayer.

Zikr

"Zikr" is the religious ceremony or act of devotion practiced by the various religious orders of "Fakirs" and "dervishes." "Zikrs" are either recited aloud or in a low voice or mentally. The most common form of "Zikr" is a recital of the ninety-nine names of God, and for those who recite them have their reward in paradise.

The Tasbih.

The Tasbih consists of ninety-nine beads and is used to facilitate the repetition of the ninety-nine names of God. In addition to the "Zikr" already mentioned, there are four others even more generally used. They are used as exclamations of joy and surprise, such as "Subhan Allah" "Holliness be to God.", Alham-do-Lilla," "Thanks, be to God", "La-ilaha-il-lal-lahu," "There is no diety but God". "Allah-Akbar," "God is Great".

The repetition of two of these sentences a hundred times, morning and evening ensures forgiveness for all venial sins.

Imams, Maulvies or Mullas.

Each Musjid has its Imam, who leads the daily prayers and is in receipt of the revenues of the Masjid, while the Moulvies and Mullahs are the teachers of the Faith, and correspond, more or less, to the doctors of divinity.

The religion of Islam comprises two essentials "Iman" or "implicit faith," and "Din" or "practical religion."

The foundations of the Islam are five in number :—

1. The recital of the "Kalima" or creed.
2. The observance of the "Namaz" or "Sula" i. e. the five prescribed periods of prayer.
3. The observance of the "Roza" or thirty days fast Ramzan.
4. The bestowal "Zakat" or alms.
5. The performance of the "Hajj" or pilgrimage to Mecca.

Of these the Kalima is by far the most important. It consists of repeating the following Arabic sentence correct as follows—"La-ilaha-Illallaho Muhammad-ur-Rasul Allah."—"There is no God but God, and Muhammad is his messenger". It is in fact, the Muslim confession of faith, and has to be repeated when anyone is converted to Islam.

Namaz or five periods of prayer.

"Namaz" is the name given to the five periods of prayer which a devout Musalman is required to observe daily. The prescribed periods are—day break, 2 o'clook in the afternoon, before sunset, after sunset and on retiring to rest.

Takbir and Rikat.

The regular form of prayer begins with the "Niyyat" or introduction which is recited in the "Quiam" or standing position, the right hand placed on the left and the eyes looking to the ground in self-abasement. Next follows the "Fateha" i. e. the recital of the first chapter of the Koran, after which come "**Takbir-i-Ruku**" and the "**Takbir-i-Sijdah**," the former repeated while making an inclination of the head and body and placing the hands upon the knees, and the latter in the attitude of "Sijdah" or prostration, in which the forehead is made to touch the ground. Then raising the head and body and sinking backward on the heels and placing the hands on the thighs, the worshipper says the "Takbir-i-Jalsa" in the "Quiam" or standing position as before. A "Takbir" in the standing position completes each "Rikat" or form of prayer.

Each "Takbir" consists of a number of pious ejaculations repeated several times such as "Allah Akbar"—"God is Great."

The "Azan" or Call to Prayer.

Namaz may be said in private or in company, or in the Masjid. The latter is considered the most meritorious and must be proceeded by the "Azan" or call to prayer recited by the "Muezzin." All prayers must be made in the direction of Kaaba.

The "Roza" or thirty days fast.

The Roza or thirty days fast take place in the month of Ramzan. The Ramzan according to Christian calendar changes about a period of ten days in each year, e. g., if it commences on the 10th day of September in one year, it will commence about the 31st of August in the following year, and so on. The fast is strictly observed from sunrise to sunset daily : the fast does not commence in the Muslim world until the new moon is seen and the news telegraphed in each country by the Imams of the "Jammia Masjid" or by the concerned department of a Muslim State. If the sky is overcast and the moon not visible, the fast commences on the completion of thirty days from the beginning of the previous month. The fast of the Ramzan should be kept by every Musalman except the sick, the aged and woman who are either pregnant or nursing their children. Soldiers on service and travellers are also exempt. In the case of a sick person or a traveller, the fast should be kept as soon as circumstances permit.

"Zakat" or alms giving.

The term Zakat literally means "purification". It is the name now given to the legal alms which every devout Musalman is enjoined by the Koran to bestow upon the poor or to devote for religious purposes. "Zakat" should be given annually on five descriptions of property, viz., money, cattle, fruit, merchandise, and land, provided the donor has been the possessor of a minimum amount of each for a year. The 2½ per cent on money, cattle, and merchandise should be given, but on land the amount may vary from 1-20th to 1-10th.

The Hajj or Pilgrimage.

The Hajj is enjoined on all Musalmans possessing the means to perform it. Pilgrimages to minor shrines of Islam are called "Ziarat" to distinguish them from the Hajj or great pilgrimage to Mecca. All Musalmans who have performed the Hajj enjoy the title of "Haji" and may wear a green turban as an outward indication of their rank.

Observances by the Masses.

All Punjabi Musalmans are, of course, observe the following principles of the religion:—

1. The performance of circumcision.

2. The five daily prayers (which cannot be said to be strictly observed by the majority).

3. The assembled prayers on Friday in a mosque.

4. The abhorrence of pork

5. Observance of the fast of Ramzan and the celebration of the Ids.

Piri Muridi

The practice is common all over the Punjab, but most

prevalent in the Upper Punjab where every single person is supposed to have a *Pir* or preceptor, who initiates him into the secrets of divine worship and guides him in his spiritual progress. No one can inspire confidence as a truthful or straightforward man until he has done "Bai'at" (affiliated himself) to some *Pir*. Once this is done, the "Murid" (disciple) depends upon the *Pir* for helping him through all his difficulties and having him absolved of all his sins. *Pirs* are a class separate from the priest or *Mulla*; Sayads are generally selected.

Ghaziz

Those who engage in war against infidels are called *Ghaziz*, and their reward is distinctly indicated in the following quotations from the Koran: "God hath indeed promised paradise to every one, but God hath preferred those that fight for the faith." And, "Those who fight in defence of God's true religion God will not suffer their works to perish".

Shahid

The title of "Shahid" or martyr is given to any one who dies as a soldier for the faith; accidentally at the hands of another; from the plague or by drowning; by the accidental fall of a wall; by burning; from hunger; through refusing to eat unlawful food; and while performing the pilgrimage to Mecca.

Fakir or Darweshes.

The word Faqir means "poor," it is used in the sense of one "poor in the sight of God" rather than "one in need of worldly assistance". *Darwesh* is applied to those who have no worldly ambitions. Both terms are generally used for those who lead religious lives. Those who attain to a high degree of sanctity are called "Pir" and "Walis", while those who attain the highest rank are called "Ghaus".

Angels.

Belief in angels is enjoined by the *Koran*. Of these the four most important are Gabriel who is God's messenger, *Michael who is the protector of the Jews*, Israfil who will sound the last trump at the final resurrection of the dead, and Azrael the angel of death. Besides the above, there are a few angels to whom special functions are allotted. The "Muaqqibit" are recorders of good and evil and are perpetually engaged in noting down a man's actions whether good or evil ? *Munkir* and *Nakir* are two angels, whose business it is to interview every man in his grave, and assertain the genuineness of his faith in Allah and His Prophet Muhammad (be peace upon him).

Devil and Ginns.

The devil is known as *Iblis* or *Shaitan*, and is considered to be fallen angel turned out of paradise because he refused to do homage to Adam. *Jinns* are really the old house hold gods worshipped before Islam in many parts of the world. *Jinns* are of two kinds—good and evil. The former extremely handsome, the latter repulsively ugly.

Prophets of Islam.

The six prophets (besides others) recongnised by Islam are Adam, Noah, Abraham, Moses, Jesus and Muhammad (be peace on all these). Each of these is supposed to have been entrusted with special mission, and to have brought new law for the guidance of mankind which successively abrogated those that preceded them. The *Koran* contain everything worthy of record contained in all previous works. It is called *Koran Sharif*, the noble *Koran*.

FOOD

A Muslim (in theory) cannot object to feed with a Christian so long as the food he eats is "halal". Any objection to do so must arise from ignorance.

Rules regarding the slaughter of animals for food.

No animal's flesh is lawful food to a Muslim unless it has been "halaled" i. e. slaughtered in the manners prescribed in the Koran, viz., by drawing a knife across the throat, and cutting the wind-pipe, the carotid arteries, and the gullet, repeating at the same time the words: "Bismillah Allah Akbar"—"In the name of the Almighty God." A clean animal so slaughtered becomes lawful food for Musalmans.

The following creatures are "Hilal" or lawful:—

1. Animals that are clovenfooted and chew the cud and are not beasts of prey.
2. Birds that do not seize their prey with their claws or wound them with their bills, but pick up food with their beaks.
3. Fish that have scales.
4. Locusts.

Horse-flesh and fish found dead in the water are generally considered unclean. Swine's flesh is held in utter abhorrence.

FESTIVALS

The Islamic year.

An account of the principal festivals of Islam may appropriately be prefaced with a list of the twelve Islamic months. The twelve lunar divisions into which Musalmans divide their year are as follows:—

1. Muharram
2. Safar
3. Rabi-ul-awal
4. Rabi-ul-akhir, or Rabi-us-sani
5. Jamadi-ul-awal
6. Jamadi-us-sani or Jamadi-ul-akhir
7. Rajab
8. Shaban
9. Ramzan
10. Shawal
11. Zul Qaudah
12. Zul Hajja

The Idul Fitar.

The *Id-ut-Fitr* or breaking on the fast forms the conclusion of the Ramazan. It is held on the first day of the month of Shawal, immediately after conclusion of the Roza. On this day after making propitiatory offering to the poor, the people assemble in the principal mosque or Musjid and proceed to the Idgah, a special place of worship, and there the *Khateeb* or priest reads the service. The prayers should be read between 7 or 8 a. m. usually. At the close of the service the members of the congregation salute and embrace each other, and returning to their homes, spend the rest of the day in feasting and merriment.

The Id-ul-Zoha or Bakr-Id.

The *Id-ul-Zoha* or *Bakrid* is held on the ninth of the month called Zul Hajja. The festival is said to commemorate Abraham's willingness to sacrifice his son Ismail ; it is the greatest Islamic festival, and is celebrated most magnificently. At this feast every Muslim who is in possession of the regulated means, i. e. seven tolas of gold or money equivalent to that, besides a house and furniture, is bound to sacrifice either a goat, or ram, or cow, or female camel in the name of God. This sacrifice is generally called Kurbani, and the flesh of the Kurbani is divided into three portions, one is reserved for the sacrificer himself : a second is given in alms to the poor and indigent ; the third is bestowed among relatives and friends.

The sacrifice of a cow or camel is held to be equivalent to that as seven goats or rams. The special reason given for the sacrifice is that those who offer up the animal will find them in readiness to assist them over the *pulsirat* or bridge which separates heaven and hell, over which all mankind will have to cross on the resurrection day. The righteous will pass over it with ease, and with the swiftness of lightning : but the wicked will miss their footing, and fall headlong into hell.

Muharram

The Muharram commence on the first of the month of that name and is continued for ten days. The period is observed by the *Shiahs* to commemorate the martyrdom of Hazrat Ali, and of Imam Hassan and Imam Hussain. The *Ashura* is also held sacred by Sunnis as it also commemorates the birth of Adam and Eve and the creation of heaven, hell, and the human race.

Muhammad (be peace upon him) enjoined on his followers the observance of ten customs during the *Muharram*, vize.,—

1. Bathing.
2. Wearing Fine apparel.
3. Allpying *Surma* to the eyes.
4. Fasting.
5. Prayers.
6. Cooking more food than usual for the poors.
7. Making peace with one's enemies, or establishing it among others.
8. Associating with pious or learned Moulvies.
9. Taking compassion on orphans, and
10. Bestowing alms.

The ceremonies of the Muharram vary greatly in different places, but the following are the main features observed by *Shiahs*. A few days before the Muharram a place is prepared called as Imambara, or Ashurkhana in the centre of which is a pit, in which fires are kindled at night. Across those fires the people fence with sticks and swords, and while dancing round them, call out "Ya Ali Shah Hassan, Shah Hussain! Hai dost! Rahio!" "Oh Ali ! Noble Hassan ! Noble Hussain ! Alas friend stays ! etc. These cries are repeated until the people reach the highest pitch of excitement. They then form themselves in a circle and beat their breasts ; while the *Maulvies* read extracts from the Rowzatul—Shahadat or Book of Martyrs.

On the seventh day of the Muharram banners are conveyed in procession and representations are made of the marriage of Kasim who married Imam Hussain's daughter on the morning of the battle of Karbela in which the latter lost his life. Commemoration, that is called *Mehndi*. On the eighth day a spear is carried about in the morning to represent Imam Hussain's head which was carried on the point of javelin, and in the evening there are processions of men carrying banners and representation of Zul-Jaunah the emblem of Imam Hussain's celebrated charger. On the ninth day it concludes with illumination and processions of *tabuts* or *Tazias* which are supposed to be models of Imam Hussain's tomb at Kerbela. They generally consist of a bamboo frame work covered over with tinsel and coloured paper, inside which are two miniature *ullums* or tombs, intended to represent those of Imam Hassan and Hussain. The last or tenth day is the Shahdat-ka-roz, or 'day of martyrdom'. On it, upto 8 p. m. the Zul-Jannah and all the *tazias* are conveyed in state from the *imambaras* to some selected place. This completes the Commemoration.

Shab-i-Barat.

The *Shab-i-Barat* is 'the night of record.' It is observed during the evening of the fifteenth day of the month of Shaban, and is so called because the Alimighty on that night registers all actions which men are to perform in the course of the ensuing year. Some Muslims often call the Shabi Barat the *Shub Quadr*, or 'night of power,' and thus confuse it with the Lylatul Quadr, a totally distinct festival which takes place on the 27th night of the month of Ramzan.

Bara Wafat.

The *Bara Wafat* commemorates the death of the Prophet (be peace upon him) which occured on the 12th of the month known as Rabbi-ul-awal. Devout Muslims assemble daily, morning and evening, either in the mosque or at their own houses and recite from the Hadis (The Hadis are records of the sayings of the Prophet (be peace upon him), and they form the oral law of the Musalman legislator and are regarded as a supplement to Korran). They also read the Buran and the Wafat-nama or story of the Prophet's (be peace upon him) death.

Akhiri Chahar Shamba.

The *Akhiri Chahar Shamba*, or last Wednesday of the month of Safar, is observed as a festival by Muslims, because the Prophet (be peace upon him), took his bath on that day on curing from sickness. Among devout Muslims it is usual on this occasion to write texts from the Koran on slips of paper, and then to wash off the ink with water, and drink the liquid to secure immunity from misfortunes. The day is observed as a holiday, and is spent in prayer.

Chapter IV

CUSTOMS AND CEREMONIES OF THE PUNJABI MUSALMANS.

1. Ceremonies relating to brith.

When a child is born the *Moulvi* is sent for and utters the call to prayer (bang or azan) in the child's ear, receiving a small present. After a few days the child's hair is cut and a name is given it and presents are made to the midwife, *moulvi* and menials. The usages are the same on the birth of both boys and girls, but the rejoicings are much greater on the birth of the former.

2. Circumcision.

Circumcision (sunnat or *Khatna karna*) is performed up to 8 or 12 years of age by the *nai* when sweetmeats are distributed and the *nai* receives a small present of money.

3. Marriage.

Marriage accoring to Islam is a sacrament and not merely a social function or a matter of convenience. Although the Musalman tribes of the Punjab are, to a large extent, of Hindu origin, Islamic Law has had such a strong effect as regards inter-marriage, that it has entirely abrogated the rule forbidding marriage between relations in fact, the endeavour is always made to arrange marriages within the circle of near relations, and marriages between first cousins are common. If it is found necessary to go further afield a bride is usually sought within the tribe, failing even that, a marriage is arranged with a girl from a tribe of equal or only slightly lower status. Punjabi Musalmans will give their daughters only to tribes of equal or higher social position. All tribes will give their daughters to *Sayyads*, keeping in mind their religious status and dignity. The only abiding rule is that in every marriage the husband's family must be at least equal in social estimation to that of the wife.

4. Betrothal

Marriage is nearly always preceded by formal betrothal (*nata, kurmai* or *mangewa*) which usually takes place between the ages of 15 and 25. After some preliminary negotiations conducted by the *nai*, or *mirasi*, or a kinsman, a date is appointed upon which the boy's father provides *gur* or *mithai*, a small sum of money, clothes for the girl, and jewels according to their station—very often a plain ring. These are placed on the head of the *nai*, who with the *mirasi* accompanies the boy's father to the girl's house. In Rawalpindi and Attock and in Shahpur a clove and some coloured thread is also sent.

The girl's father takes the *gur* or *mithai* inside, and the *nai* takes care of the rest. That night the girl's father gives a feast to the boy's father and others, and next morning the girl's relations assemble and feast the guests, and place the *gur* or *mithai* sent by the boy's father, before all the relations of the girls. The other articles—clothes, jewels, clove, etc., etc., taken charge of by the *nai* are placed in a *thal* or open vessel, and set before the girl's relatives. The *Mullah* then comes forward and prays for a blessing on the betrothal (*dua khair*) which sometimes repeated three times. The *gur* or *mithai* then divided amongst all present and all the other articles are taken by the girl's relatives. In some districts one rupee is placed in the girl's hand as a token (*nishan*). Presents are made to the *Mullah, nai,* and *mirasi,* and the boy's father and relatives then take leave. The clove bought by them, coloured with saffron, is at the same time returned by the girl's father to the boy's father. Occasionally, too, *purgis* are given to some of those accompanying the boy's father. The girl's father then feeds his own relatives and dismiss them. The girl's female relatives at this time sing songs of rejoicing.

On the 'Id following, the boy's parents send a present of clothes, ornaments and money and some eatables, according to their status, for the girl.

Others do without any formal ceremony except that of having the *"dua khair"* recited in the presence of the assembled relatives. It is not usual to write out a contract of betrothal.

5. Marriage

The date "ukad" of the actual marriage is fixed at another meeting, accompanied by ceremonies, and courtesies arranged at the instance of the boy's father. After fixing the date the parents of both parties despatch presents of *gur, methai* etc, to their more distant relatives and friends by the hands of the *nai*, who receives small presents of money, or of grain at each house. This practice is known as sending the *"gandh"*

A week before the wedding, the ceremony of enointing with oil is performed. In the afternoon the female relatives and those of the *mirasi* assemble and sing at the houses of the bride and bridegroom. They place each of the betrothed, at their respective houses, upon an inverted basket in the yard of the house and four women hold a canopy over his or her head.

From that date until after the wedding the betrothed do no work but get good food. The women of both the houses assemble and sing.

Then comes the ceremony of bathing the bridegroom. On the morning of the *"barat"* (marriage procession) the potter's wife brings an earthen vessel. The waterman fills it, this is called "gharah garauli" The *Mussali* or sweeper then prepares and brings a *Kharah* or basket, turns it upside down, puts the bridegroom on it, and lights a lamp under it. The bridegroom is then bathed by the village servants with the water from the *gharah*, the whole brotherhood, male and female, standing around. In Shahpur the brother bridegroom's sister or niece siezes his sheet and is bribed with a present to let it go. In Rawalpindi the *nai* places water in the bridegroom's hand, who scatters it to the four cardinal points, signifying his desire to include all in happiness similar to his own.

On getting up off his seat the bridegroom crushes with his right foot the earthenware lid of jar, this is supposed to avert the "evil eye." The dirty clothes worn by the bridegroom are then taken by the *nai* as his perquisite, and the bridegroom is clothed in new graments.

The order of the foregoing ceremonies is sometimes altered Then comes the receiving of the wedding presents (*neundra*). The wedding procession (*barat or janj*) is then formed and proceeds to the village of the bride. In various districts of the Punjab before the departure of the *barat* the bridegroom's sister offers grain to his horse and holts its halter, for which she received a present. The party on arrival at the village of the bride is received by the respectable people of the village. The party adjourns to some large building arranged for the purpose., where the bride's father gives a feast to the guests, fakirs, beggars, etc. Then certain of the guests accompaning the bridegroom and his father enter into the house carrying trays of present. After this the marriage contract (*nika*) is performed by the *Maulvi*. The bride's elders answer for her and the bridegroom answers for himself.

A display is then made of the bride's dower (*daj*). After that the barat conveys the tribe to the bridegroom's house. She remains there for two or three days and she then returns to her parents. Her husband later on goes in procession (*bedah*) to fetch her home for good.

Marriage customs differ slightly according to the tribe or locality, but the foregoing gives some idea of the main observance. Amongst Muslims marriage nearly always takes place of puberty and the bride goes to live with her husband at once, other-wise she lives with her parents till of fit age.

Expense of Marriages.

Marriages are usually very extravagant, each stage of the whole ceremony being marked by feasts and presentations by either or both parties, and the *mirasis* and menials of both parties reap a rich harvest of gifts. Thus the average expense of wedding ranges from Rs. 1000/- to Rs.50,000.00 or more according to the status of the parties. An endavour has been made to reduce the marriage expenditure and recently law is framed to minimise the expenses made on dowree (Jahez)).

6. Marriage Seasons.

There is no special time or season for marriages, but they are forbidden during the month of Muharram, on the 'Ids, during the first thirteen days of Safar.

7. Widow re-marriage

The *'Shara'* (Islamic Law) does not forbid the marriage of widows and the general custom amongst Muslims does not enforce widowhood.

8. Marriage Contract.

At no age can a women enter into a contract for her own marriage. The contract of betrothal is revocable at any time before the actual *Nikah*.

9. marriage within the tribe.

Among Punjabi Musalmans marriages are generally confined to one's own tribe, sub-tribe or caste, and where possible, alliances are arranged between the brothers and sisters, offspring as a means of retaining the same family, the property inherited by the boy and the girl. Marrying outside one's own caste or tribe is not against Islamic Law.

TERMS OE RELATIONSHIP

Father	... Bap, Walid or Piu
Mother	... Man or Ma
Father's Father	... Dada
Father's Young brother	... Chacha
Father's sister	... Phupi or Bua
Father's sister's husband	... Phuphar
Mother's sister	... Masi

Mother's brother	... Mama
Mother's brother's wife	... Mami
Mother's father	... Nana
Mother's mother	... Nani
Mother's father's father	... Parnana
Mother's mother's mother	... Parnani
Father-in-law	... Susra or Saohra
Mother-in-law	... Sas or Sass
Wife's brother	... Sala
Wife's sister	... Sali
Wife's sister husband	... Sandu
Daughter	... Beti
Son	... Beta or Putr
Sister's child	... Bhanja or Bhanji
Brother's child	... Bhattija or Bhattiji

Burial Ceremonies.

Funerals—At funerals the services prescribed in the *Koran* are followed. The grave is dug with a recess (*same*) along the western side, in which the body is placed with its face towards the south. Bricks and stones are then placed leaning over the corpse so that no earth may rest on it.

Before the burial the Imam recites the burial service (*janaza*) accompanied by the mourners, and after the burial alms are given to the poor. The Imam is presented with a copy of the *Koran* and a small money present.

On the third day after the funeral the relations read the "*Kul*" and distribute food to those who came to condole with them. This completes the obligatory period of mourning, the full period according to the *Koran* is forty days.

Language.

With the exception of the *Mishwanis* of the Hazara district, the universal language is *Punjabi*, but each tract has its own dialects. These dialects shade off imperceptibly into one another and the residents of one tract are intelligible to those of any other tract.

Manners and Gestures.

When friends meet they join hands, or if they are great friends, they embrace each other breast to breast, first one side and then the other. If a man meets a holy person he kisses the latter's hands by way of salutation. Should acquaintances pass each other, one says "Salam alaikum" (peace be unto thee) and the other replies "Wa Alaikum ussalam" (and on thee be peace). They then enquire after each other's health the usual question being "is it well" (*khair*) and the answer "fairly" (*val*) or "thank to God" (*shukr*). When a visitor comes to a house he is saluted with a welcome جی آیا نوں "a'ji aea nun" and answers "Blessings be on thee" (*khair howi*) - خیر ہوی

The salam *and salutations.*—When a person makes a "*salam*" and any of the assembly rise and return it, it is considered sufficient for the whole company. The lesser number should always salute the greater, he who rides should salute him who walks, he who walks to him who stands, the stander the sitter, and so on. A man should not salute a woman on the road. Salutes should be made with the right hand.

Salams are of various kinds, the ordinary *salam* among equals consists of merely touching the forhead with the right hand. "*Bandugi*" is very much the same, except that the head is inclined gently forward so as to meet the hand. "*Kurnish*" كورنش is the same as the latter but the body is bent as well as the head. "*Taslimat*" تسلیمات consists in touching the ground with the finger and then making "*salam*". It is generally repeated thrice before the Kings (that is the custom of old days, and not now) "*Gale milna*" is the form of salutation usual among intimate friends who embrace each other by throwing their arms across each other's necks, and in that position incline the head three times, first on one-shoulder and then on the other. Homage or "*Kadm bosi*" قدم بوسی is paid by kissing the feet of the ruler or the edge of the carpet, on which he stands. Soldiers or persons allowed to bear arms, generally offer their swords to superiors as a "*nazzar*" or offering of their services. The person saluted signifies his acceptance of the gift by touching the hilt of the weapon. Homage in some countries is sometimes paid by casting the turban at the feet of the conqueror; a man who wishes to throw himself on one's mercy and asks for clemency, will sometimes do this. Touching the knee of the person saluted is often the sign of affectionate respect. (This old Hindu custom is now no more anywhere in Punjab.

Gestures.—Some of their gestures are peculiar: although as in Europe, a nod of the head means "yes" or "come" and a shake of the head means denial. Thus a backward nod means enquiry; a click of the tongue with a toss of the head means "no"; jerking the fingers inwards means "I do not know"; holding the palm inwards and shaking the hand means enquiry, holding the palm outwards and shaking the hand is a sign of prohibition, holding up the thumb (*thutth*) means contemptuous refusal ; wagging the middle finger (*dhiri*) provokes a person to anger, and holding up the open palm is a great insult. In beckoning to a person the hand is held up palm outwards and the fingers moved downwards and inwards.

Laws of Inheritance.

Although the question of inheritance is dealt with by Muslim law, most Musalmans adhere to their tribal customs which are generally those of the races from which they were originally converted. In many parts of the Punjab, succession to landed property is regulated by two rules, *viz.*, "*Pagriband*" when the estate is divided equally among the sons irrespective of the number of wives, and "*chadarband*" when the property is divided among the wives so that each family may come in for a share. Where there are sons, daughters receive nothing and widows are only entitled to maintenance. Where there are no sons, a widow may have a life interest in the property, which would afterwards descend either to a daughter, or to a distant collateral in the male line. Daughters very seldom succeed to landed property, and when they do, it is necessary that the land should have been given as a dowry, or formally bestowed during the life-time of the father. An illegitimate son cannot inherit. A son, however, by a woman whom the father could not have legally married, such as a dancing girl, a prostitute, or a woman of very low caste, cannot inherit under any circumstances. Adoption is very rare among Muslim. It is only permissible on the failure of issue, and even then must be proclaimed openly by the adopter during his life time and supported by the written deed.

Food and Drink, Cloths, Personal Habits etc., etc.

The Punjabi Musalman has usually two meals a day,—first inthe morning and second in the evening. Lunch (mid-day meal) is familier in the cities. If a cultivator has some hard work in hand, he generally eats some of the food left over from the previous night, before starting for his daily toil. His morning meal, which consists of three or four cakes made of wheat, barley and gram or *jowar* is sometimes brought to him in the fields but is more often eaten at home, as the woman being secluded, are unable to leave their houses. The evening meal consist of *roti, i. e., chapatis,* pulses, *i. e. dal,* lentils, etc., vegetables and a few relishes, such as salt, pepper, chillies, and curry-stuffs, with *masala* or various kinds of condiments. As a change, most Muslims, eat rice, *khichri, i.e.,* rice or *"bajra"* mixed with *dal, dhai* or curds, eggs, fish and enormous quantities of sugarcane whenever procurable. Meat is too expensive a luxury to be indulged in more than occasionally, but when it is procurable, it is served in various forms, such as *pillaos, kabbabs* and curries. *Lassi* or butter-milk is an important article of diet, particularly among Jats. At the *Bakr-Id* and on the occasions of rejoicing, such as births and marriages, even the poorest classes manage to sacrifice a goat or *dumba, i. e.,* fat-tailed sheep.

The usual beverages are water, milk, and sherbets.

All kinds of drugs and liquor are forbidden in the *Koran.* Some Muslims however, indulge in the former "sub rosa", and the use of the latter in the form of *charas, bhang* and opium, is very prevalent. *Charas* (the exudation of the flowers of hemp, collected with the dew, and prepared for use as an intoxicating drug) is generally mixed with the tobacco of the *huka* and smoked, –*bhang* (made with the leaves of the hemp plant) is taken in a liquid form.

Smoking is universal, and the *huka* is always within easy reach.

Clothes—The usual garments are a *majla* or loin cloth worn round the waist like a kilt, a *kurta* or loose skirt sometimes confined by a *kammarband*, a *chadar* or wrapper and a turban or *pag* which varies in size and colour according to the rank of the wearer. The *pagri* and *majla* of the well-to-do classes is usually white, but Jats, Gujars, and Baluchis, delight in coloured garments, blue being their favourite dye. The wealthy and educated classes are taking more and more to clothes fashioned on the English pattern. *Salwar*, *Kameez* and *Achkan* is the National dress.

Hospitality to strangers is enjoined by the *Koran* and is a marked characteristic of the Punjabi Muslims. Travellers are lodged in the *hujra* or guest-house of which every village possesses at least one or two. Guests are fed at the public expense and their wants are attended to by the *Kamins* or village servants. The *hujra* besides being a resting place for travellers, is a place of public resort where the male population of the village meet in the evening to discuss affairs.

Personal habits.—Although the *Koran* enjoins personal cleanliness, majority do not pay as much attention to their ablutions as instructed.

Ablutions are of two kinds, *viz.*, *wazu* or washing the face, hands and feet, etc., which is necessary before every kind of prayer, and *ghusal* or washing the whole body after certain defilements.

Besides the ablutions prescribed by their religion, Muslims observe certain practices called *"fitrat"* which have been prevalent among Arabs since the time of Abraham. The more important of these are the clipping of the moustache, so that the hair may not enter the mouth; not cutting or shaving the beard; cleaning the teeth; cleaning the nostrils with water at the usual ablutions; cutting the nails; cleaning the finger joints; pulling out the hair under the arms; and a few similar customs.

Amusement and Games.

Although the agriculturist of the Punjab leads a hard laborious life as a rule, he allows himself a certain amount of time for recreation. Attendance at weddings and other domestic celebrations afford one means of breaking the monotony of his life, and a fair or two are probably visited in the course of the year.

Pir kaudi.—There are also games of various kinds, though the extent to which these are indulged in, varies a good deal in different localities. The best known game is called *"Pirkaudi"*. The competitors in this game form groups at two sides of a square where they are surrounded by their respective friends and backers. One man (*bahari*) is selected from a side and advances into the arena—this is the challenger of all comers. Two opponents (*andari*) are selected and advance against the challenger, their object being to throw the challenger over and make his back and shoulders touch the ground, while he tries to tackle one at a time and do likewise. The opponents of the challenger, however, are not allowed to commence their attack until he has touched them. To keep his opponents off, the challenger is allowed to slap, push or throw them over or to trip them up in any way he can, and dodge away before they can touch him. If the two succeed in throwing the challenger, their side have to send out a man as challenger, and so the game continues until the champion is determined.

Saunchi.—In some parts another form of *kaudi* is played called "*saunchi*". Two men stand facing each other bare-breasted, one hits the other with his open palm the whole game consisting in his endeavour to do so without letting his opponent seize his wrist.

Lambi Kaudi and Kaudi Kabadi.—These are quite different from "*pir kaudi*" and are kinds of "prisoner's base."

Chappan chott and Lukchhip.— These are the same as "Hide and Seek."

Kanhuritala.—Correspondence to tipcat.

Chinji tarap.—This is a form of "Hopscotch".

Gulli danda.—Is very like hockey.

There are various other games of a similar kind to the above.

Bagdar uthana or Tarar ultan.—This consists in the lifting of heavy weights.

Mungli pherna.—This is the working of heavy Pak clubs.

Putting the stone also arouses great interest and competition.

The old men play *"Chaupatt,"* a game something similar to backgammon played with dice (*kauri*), and some play chess *"Shatranj."*

A favourite card game is *"tash"*. This is somewhat similar to *whist* and is played with 51 cards, the deuce of diamonds being discarded.

Shikar with long dogs is most popular in Rawalpindi, Shahpur and Mianwali Districts.

SUPERSTITIONS

In matters pertaining to his superstitions, the Punjabi Musalman now does not belive much in fabulous tales due to general rise in education. But illitrate are yet superstitions. It is not so long ago that an individual in the Rawalpindi district, extracted large sums of money out of the inhabitants of his *tahsil* by claiming the power to double any money placed in his charge. In very recent years a belief that the foxhounds in Peshawar were periodically fed on criminals, who were actually "thrown to the dogs," was prevalent.

Those who live in the hills are possibly more superstitious than the plains folk, a similar fact being observed by Buckle in his "Civilisation in Europe."

"The evil eye," talisman, amulets lucky and unlucky days, etc., etc., all have a real significance to the Punjabi Musalman. Horses and cattle may have lucky and unlucky Marks. Certain marks branded on an animal may improve it, for instance, a very sluggish horse can be turned into a spirited animal if a line is branded horizont-

ally round its body, the idea being that the animal will always be endeavouring to jump out of this mark.

There are numerous *Pirs* or saints who have the power of preventing hydrophobia in any one who has been bitten by a mad dog or jackal.

Visits to different *Ziarats* or shrines are often undertaken for a specific object connected with the supposed power in the shrine to cure certain ailments.

Many localities are supposed to be haunted, and no one will go near them after dark. Instances have actually occurred where sentries have been overcome by fear owing to this belief.

The belief in the *evil eye* is universal. An amulet (*tawiz*) containing a verse from the *Koran*, is worn as a protection against the *evil eye*. This is worn round the arm, the neck, or tied up in the end of the *pugri* Every carpet or piece of embroidery will have a small portion of it which is out of harmony with the pattern as a protection against the *evil eye*.

Journeys.—Tuesdays and Wednesdays are unlucky days and Mondays and Fridays are lucky days on which to start on a journey, northwards. For a southward journey Thursday is a bad day and Wednesday a good day on which to start. Monday and Saturday are bad and Sunday and Tuesday good for an eastward journey. For a westward journey Sunday and Thursday are bad and Monday and Saturday good.

On starting on a journey it is fortunate to meet someone carrying water, a sweeper, a dog, a woman with a child, a maiden, all kinds of flowers, a *mali*, a donkey, a *Raja*, a horseman, a drum or anyone who is carrying a vessel containing milk, curds, *ghi*, vegetables or sugar.

It is considered unlucky to meet a *Brahman*, a man with a bare head, any person weeping, a crow flying towards one, a broken vessel in a person's hand, a cat, a *mali* with an empty basket, a goat or cow or any black animal, a snake, or an empty *gharah* carried by someone. To hear the sound of crying or sneezing while on a journey is most unlucky.

Enquires as to a man's tribe, sub-tribe, etc., etc.—To find out a man's clan, sub-section or sub-tribe, is some times difficult, owing to the various meanings of the words "zat," "got," "kom," etc.

"Zat" and "kom" are usual for the tribe, *i. e.*, "teri ki zat" or "ki kom," the man then gives the name of his tribe, *viz.*, Awan, Gakhar, Dhund, or Tanaoli, etc., and the next question would generally be "kera Awan" or "kera Gakkhar"; this should elicit the answers:—Admal, Sarangal, etc., etc., or "Kutbshahi" for the Awan. If further information is required, the questions would take the form of "kis Khandan se hai" or "teri ki walhai" or "kis pusht se chala hai," etc., depending on the tribe the man belongs to or the part of the country he comes from.

Chapter V

DISTRIBUTION OF TRIBES,

Short accounts of Punjabi Musalman tribes of Rajput, Jat, Gujar and others.

1. Alpials.

1. *Male population.*—Approximately 4,500. (Census 1931).

2. *Locality*—The Alpials occupy a compact block of villages on both banks of the Sohan river, in the Sil Sohan circle of the Fatehjang tahsil, Attock district.

3. *Headman.*—The recognised head of the tribe belong to the family of the Chaudris of Chakri.

5. *History and particulars.*—The alpials have recorded themselves as Manj Rajputs, and their claim to Rajput origin is generally admitted. They appear to have settled in their present locality about the same time as the Jodhras and Ghebas, *i, e.*, about the 15th Century, having first wandered through the country now contained in the Khushab and Talagang tahsils before settling down in the southern corner of Fatehjang.

The Alpials are hardworking and excellent cultivators, generally tilling their own land, and working laboriously on their own wells. Socially they rang high, and they inter-marry freely with the Ghebas.

They are reported to be a bold and courageous,

Sturdy, independent, and wonderfully quarrelsome. Their physique is fair, the men being somewhat light and of medium stature.

2. Andwal.

1. *Male population.*—About 1,300 (Census 1931)

2. *Locality.*—The Andwal are found in the Abbottabad tahsil of the Hazara district.

3. *Particulars.*—The Andwal are classed by Sir Denzil Ibbetson as being a section of the Dhunds.

They endeavour, at times to pass themselves off as Hindwals, which is a section of the Tanaolis.

3. Arains.

Male population.—7,26,913 (Census 1931)

The Arains or Rains are a Musalman agricultural tribe, good cultivators, skilful, industrious, hardy and thrifty.

The Arains claim to have come originally from Arabia, to have settled in Sind, thence spread to Uch in Upper Sind, and later migrated to the Punjab by way of Multan and Sirsa. They may be designated as a fighting race which has produced many Civil and Military Officers who have rendered good services to the nation.

4. Awan.

1. *Male population.*—2,88,310 (Census 1931)

2. *Locality.*—Awans are found throughout the Punjab, but their characteristics, physique and social

status vary greatly in each district. They are at their best in the Salt Range and in the districts adjoining it.

3. *Leading Families.*—All Awans of the Salt Range acknowledge the Malik of Kalabagh as their head. Other well-known families are to be found in Lawa, Kund, Kufri, Tamman, Monara, Kallar Kahar, and Buchal Kalan.

History and particulars.—The Awans claim Arab descent from Kutb Shah of Ghanzi, who ruled at Herat, but joined Sultan Mahmud of Ghaznavi in his invasions of India (1001 A. D.) and received from him the name of Awan or "helper". Kutb Shah was descended from Hazrat Ali, the son-in-law of the *Prophet*, (Peace be upon him) and the Awans have been Musalmans from the beginning; Kutb Shah had six sons:—

Kalan Shah—who settled near Kalabagh,

Gauhar Shah— who settled near Sakesur,

Chohan Shah—who settled in the hills near the Indus,

Khokhar Shah—who settled in the country about the Chenab,

Tori Shah and Jhajh Shah—who remained in the trans-border country where their descendants are said still to live in Tirah and the Kurram Valley.

Doubt has been thrown on this account by some ethnological authorities and a Hindu orgin has been assigned to the Awans by some writers, who point to the originally Hindu character of two of Kutb Shah's sons,

Chohan and Khokhar, which is not explained away by the tradition that these two sons took their mother's name. A more precise version of the Awan legend, which obtains among the Awans of Kapurthala, make them Alwi Sayads who, oppressed by the Abbassides, sought refuge in Sindh and eventually allied them-selves with Sabukhtagin (Father of Mahmud of Ghaznavi), who bestowed on them the title of Awan. They may, according to this tradition, possibly have come into Sindh with the first Arab invaders and have worked their way north. It is beyond question that they found the Janjuas in possession of the Western Salt Range and ejected them.

The above explanation of their origin, by the Awan and others, has been rejected by Pandit Harikishan Kaul in his report on the census of 1911. Pandit Harikishan Kaul considers the evidence in favour of the Hindu origin of the Awans to be too strong to set aside. He points out that the name Awan is the unalloyed Sanskrit term "Awan" meaning defender or protector. Moreover, the tribe still retains strong traces of Indian customs. He considers that it is probable that they have, from time immemorial, been located in the tract north of the Salt Range and that they received the title Awan in the Hindu times, owing to the successful defence of their stronghold against aggression. Further at a much later date, *i.e.*, after the Muhammadan invasions, they seem to have been converted by Syad Kutb Shah, after which the Awans began to call themselves Kutb Shahi, *i.e.*, the followers of Kutb Shah.

The Awans are divided into numerous clans (Muhi) which take their name from the common ancestor. Thus the Mumnals are descended from Moman, the Saghrals from Saghar, and the Shials from Shehan, and so on.

The following are the best known of these clans :—

Khokhar	Rehan	Darhal	Saghral	Chajji
Mumnal	Jand	Gulshahi	Shial	Saidan
Khattar	Babkal	Kang	Sudkal	Parbal
Kalgan	Khurana	Chohan	Bugdial	Ballial

But besides these there are over 700 sub-castes of Awans. It is seldom that any Awan will mention one of these as his clan, he will inveriably say that he is a Kutab Shahi Awan.

6. *Political factions.*—The Awans of the Salt Range are divided into two well-known political factions or parties :—Ujjal Khan's party and Khan Beg's party. Every village has its adherents of each party. The parties intermarry freely, but yet they are antagonistic to one another and will always take sides with their faction in any dispute.

The Awans have possessed political importance for a considerable period of time in the Salt Range and in the adjoining districts, and it is here that the best material for the Army is to be obtained.

In the Salt Range the Awans are described as being a brave, high-spirited people with frank, engaging manners, at the same time headstrong and irascible to an unusual degree.

Their characteristic failings are vindictiveness and a proneness to keep alive old feuds. As a rule they do not give their daughter in marriage to other tribes except to Sayads. They abstain from marriage in the same *got* or *sept*.

5. Bachharas.

1. *Male Population.*—Approximately 2,000 (Census 1931).

2. *Locality.*—The South East border of the Mianwali district. Their chief village is Wan Bucharan.

3. *Headman.*—The most influential man of the tribe is a Zaildar. His son was given a direct commission in a cavalary regiment.

4. *History and particulars.*—The Bachhars are Khokhar Rajputs. They state that their original home was in the Gujrat district, whence they moved, first to Buggi Bhooki near Girot in Shahpur, and later to their present site, which was chosen on account of the "wan" or large well built by Sher Shah. These wells were placed at intervels of about a day's march apart on the road from Gujrat to Bannu and the frontier.

The name "Bachhar" seems to have been a form of endearment applied to them by some forgotten 'Pir".

Their circumstances have been much changed of late, owing to their discovery that the soil of "thal" was most suitable for the cultivation of gram : they are now very well-off. In appearence and general characteristics they resemble the people of the Shahpur district.

6. Badhal.

This small tribe is supposed to be allied to Bhakral, but the members of the tribe itself do not agree to this. Like the Bhakral, they are said to have come across from Jammu territory. The tribe to classed as Rajput, but it does not hold a very high social position. They are of fine physique and good cultivators. They enlist freely and make good soldiers.

7. Badhan.

1. *Male population.*—3,000 (Census 1931).

2. *Locality.*—Found chiefly in Jammu and Poonch, a few are met with in the Sialkot district.

3. *Particulars.*—In Poonch the tribe is reported to have originally been weavers.

The Badhans utterly deny that they were ever weavers and claim to be Janjaus. Some of the tribe also claim connection with the Sudhans, but the Sudhans look them with contempt. They share a few villages with the Sudhans in Poonch.

8. Baghial and Bangial

1. *Male population.*—Approximately 2,000 (Census 1931).

2. *Locality.*—The tribe is found chiefly in the Rawalpindi district, where they occupy five villages in the Gujar Khan tehsil. There appear to be a few also in the Jhelum, Gujrat and Gujranwala districts

3. *Particulars.*—The Baghial and Bangial appear to be the same tribe, those members of it which are in the Rawalpindi district are classed as Rajputs, while in Gujrat, Gujranwala and Jhelum they are Jats. They describe themselves as being Punwar Rajputs. The first ancestor of Musalman faith was Bangash Khan.

They enlist freely and make good soldiers

The tribe is not to be confused with the Bagial section of the Gakkhars with whom they have no connection.

9. Bajwa and Bajju.

1. *Male population.*—3,500 (Census 1931).

2. *Locality.*—The Bajwa are found mostly in the Sialkot district, but also in the Multan district.

3. *Chief families.*—The families of the Chaudhri of Chakwandi and Khanawali in the Zaffarwal tahsil of the Sialkot district, are the most important.

4. *History and particulers.*—The Bajju ranks as Rajput and the Bajwa as Jat. Both branches have given their name to the Bajwat or country at the foot of the Jammu hills in the Sialkot district.

They say they are Solar Rajputs and that their ancestor, Raja Shalip was driven out of Multan in the time of Sakandar Lodi. The Bajju Rajputs are said to marry their daughters to the Chibs and Manhas Rajputs.

In their betrothals, dates are used, and custom purhaps brought from Multan. The Bajwa inter-marry with all the principal Jat tribes.

10. Baluch.

1. *Male population.*—3,41,544 (Census 1931).

2. *Locality.*—The Montgomery, Shahpur, Mianwali,

Jhang, Multan, Muzaffargarh, and Dera Ghazi Khan districts, Bahawalpur State and the Chenab Colony.

3. *Chief families.*—In the Shahpur district there are two families of importance, one in Sahiwal which is mentioned in the "Punjab Chiefs" and another in Khushab.

4. *History and particulars.*—The Baluchis claim Arabian extraction, asserting that they are descended from Amir Hamza an ancle of the *Praphet* (ﷺ) (peace be upon him) and from a fairy (Pari).

They consistently place their first settlement in Alleppo, from which they were expelled in A. D. 680 by Yazid, the second of the Ommayyad Caliphs.

Their migration took them first to Karman, then to Sistan, and finally, a great portion of the race, into the Punjab plains about the 13th century. Their claim to Arabian descent has generally been allowed.

About the beginning of the 16th century the Baluchis were driven out of the Khelat valley by the Brahuis and Turks. Yielding to pressure they moved eastward into the Sulaimans, drove out the Pathans, and settled along the banks of the Indus. Three Baluch adventurers Ismail Khan, Fatteh Khan, and Ghazi Khan, founded the three Dehras that bear their names, and established themselves as independent rulers of the Lower Derajat and Muzaffargarh, which they and their descendants held for nearly 300 years. Thence the southern Baluchis gradually spread into the valleys of the Indus, Chenab, and Sutlej, and in 1555 a large body of Baluchis, under their great leader Mir Chakar, accompanied the Emperor Humayun into India. It is probable that many of the Baluch settlements, in the Eastern districts of the Punjab, were founded by Humayun's soldiers. Mir Chakar settled in Sahiwal and his tomb still exists at Satgarha, where he founded a military colony of "Rinds."

Long before Mir Chakar's time, Mir Jalal Khan was one of the Baluch historical rulers, and from his four sons —Rind, Lashar, Hot and Korai spring the four main Baluch tribes. The Jatoi are the children of Jatoi, Jalal Khan's daughter. These main sections are now divided into innumerable septs. Throughout the Punjab the term Baluch denotes any Muslim camel-man. The word has come to be associated with the care of camels, because the Baluch settlers of the Western plains have taken to the grazing and breeding of camels rather than to husbandry, and every Baluch is supposed to be a camel-man and every camel-man to be a Baluch.

The Baluch of the Punjab plains is now altogether separated from the Baluch tribes of Baluchistan and the Derajat, although the same tribal names are still found among them. Long residence in Punjab and inter-marriage with the Jats has deprived them of many of their national characteristics, and they have now forgotten the Baluch language and have abandoned the Baluch dress.

They are good Muslims, fair agriculturists, and make good soldiers. In proportion to their population the number that enlist in the army as well as in the civil is small.

In character they are brave, chivalrous, and honourable. In physique they are tall, thin, wiry, hardy, and frugal in their habits.

The following clans are those most commonly found in the Cis-Indus districts of the Punjab :—

| Korai | Gopand | Muhori | Rind | Gurmani | Dashti |
| Jatai | Gishkauri | Mazari | Hot | Pitafi | Zangeza |

The Rind, Jatoi and Korai are numerous in Multan, Jhang, Sahiwal, Shahpur and Muzaffargarh districts.

The Gopangs are a servile tribe as also are the Dashtis, both are found in the Muzaffargarh district.

The Hot are found in Jhang, Multan and Muzaffargarh.

The Gurmanis, Giskhauris, Pitafis in Muzaffargarh. The Mazaris in Jhang. The Zangeza are met with in the Mianwali and Shahpur districts. They are Shiahs. The Magassi Baluch, who are found in Multan, Muzaffargarh, Mianwali and Jhang, appear to be a "peculiar people" rather than a tribe. Both Sunnis and Shiahs are found among them and they have several peculiar customs not to be found among other Baluchis.

The Baluchis of the Punjab inter-marry with the Jats.

11. Bambas.

Though few in numbers the Bambas are an important tribe in Kashmir, where they are chiefly found in the Muzaffarabad district between the Jhelum and Kishenganga rivers.

They are represented in the Boi tract of the Munsehra

tahsil of Hazara by two families, one of Boi and the other of Jabri Kalish. The Boi family, is one of great importance in the Hazara district, second only to the Amb family of Tanawal.

12. Bhakral.

1. *Population.*— 6,600. (Census 1931)

2. *Locality.*—In the Gujar Khan and Rawalpindi tahsils of the Rawalpindi district, also a few villages in the Chakwal tahsil of the Jhelum district.

3. *Chief families.*—There are several pensioned Military officers belonging to the tribe notably at Saba Mora in the Chakwal Tahsil (Jhelum) and Kamtrila in the Gujar Khan tahsil (Rawalpindi).

4. *History and particulars.* - The Bhakral claim to be Punwar Rajputs, and since the 1901 census was taken, a large number have returned themselves as such. They probably came from Jammu territory across the Jhelum river. The tribe now ranks as Rajput and appears to hold a high place in the social scale. They do not appear to marry outside the tribe. They are good cultivators, of fine physique, fond of military service, and make excellent soldiers.

13. Bhatti.

1. *Population in the Punjab.*—Rajput.—319,800, Jat. 41,500. (census 1931).

2. *Locality.*—The Bhattis are found throughout the Punjab, but are most numerous in the Lahore, Multan, Rawalpindi, Gujranwala and Sialkot districts.

3. *History and particulars.* The Bhatti is one of the best known of the Rajput clans, the modern representatives of the ancient Yadubansi Rajputs, and supposed to be the "Baternae" mentioned by Pliny.

Their traditions connect the tribe with Bikaner, Jaisalmer and the old fortress of Bhatner. In each locality appear variations of the story of their origin. The most common story is that they were driven across the Indus, from the East, in very early times, and that they returned across the river some 700 years ago, when they took possession of the country to the south of the lower Sutlej. The tribe gives its name to the Bhattiana, and to the Bhattiora tracts, as well as to various places such as Bhatinda, Bhatner, Pindi Bhattian, etc.

The various branches of the Bhatti differ in social status and characteristics according to the locality in which they are found.

Probably the best representatives of the tribe are now to be found in the Bhattiora tract north of the Chenab (in the Sarghoda tahsil and the Chiniot tahsil of Jhang). Here, they are "fine race of men, industrious agriculturists, good horse breeders, and very fond of sports" and they have also now proved themselves good soldiers.

In the Gujar Khan tahsil of the Rawalpindi district there are also to be found good represenetatives of the tribe.

The Bhattis of Gujranwala enjoyed considerable political importance and still hold 86 villages in that district. The Bhattis of the Sialkot district will not give their daughters in marriage to any of the neighbouring tribes. In the Salt Range the Bhatti seem to hold ordinary position.

Muslim Bhattis were converted about the end of the 15th century.

14. Chaddar.

1. *Population.*—Jat—17,000, Rajput—3,600. (census 1931).

2. *Locality.*—The tribe is found along the whole length of the Chenab and Ravi valleys, but is most numerous in the Chenab Colony and Jhang.

3. *History and particulars.*—The Chaddars of Jhang claim to be Rajputs, elsewhere they rank as Jats.

They say that they left their original home in Rajputana in the time of Muhammad of Ghor and settled in Bahawalpur, where they were converted by Sher Shah of Uch. Thence they came to Jhang, where they founded an important colony and spread in smaller numbers up the Chenab and Rabi. The Chadder are of Tunwar Rajput origin.

Their chief sub-tribes are :—

The Rajokes, Kamokes, Jappas, Luns, Pajiken, Deokes, Bullankes, and Sajokes.

They are described as being good agriculturists.

The name of this tribe is better represented by the spelling *Chaddrar*.

15. Chattha.

1. *Population.*—4,600. (census 1931).

2. *Locality.*—This tribe is chiefly found in the Gujranwala district, and also in small numbers scattered about the central Punjab.

3. The Chattha is a Jat tribe. They claim Chauhan Rajput descent. From Chattha, a grand-son of Prithi Raj, the Chauhan King of Delhi. Some 500 years ago, Dahru came from Shambhal in Moradabad, where the bards of the Karnal Chauhan still live, to the banks of the Chenab, and married among the Jat tribes of Gujranwala. They were converted to Islam about 1600 A. D. The tribe rose to considerable importance under the Sikhs, and their leading family is mentioned in the "Punjab Chiefs."

16. Chauhan.

1. *Population in the Punjab.*—71,000. (census 1911).

2. *Locality.*—Chiefly found in the Amballa and Karnal districts, in small numbers in the Lahore, Jhulem, Rawalpindi and Multan districts.

3. *Particulars.*—The Chauhan is one of the 36 royal Rajput tribes. Pirthi Raj, the last Hindu ruler of Hindustan, was of this tribe. Ajmer and Sambhar seem to have been their original home before they moved to Delhi. In the Punjab they now retain their dominant position. They are found scattered throughout the Punjab. Many tribes of doubtful status claim to be Chauhans.

17. Chib.

1. *Male population in the Punjab and Jammu.*—10,800. (census 1931).

2. *Locality.*—This tribe is found chiefly in the Kharian tahsil of Gujrat, and also in the adjacent territory of Jammu.

3. *Chief families.*—The Pothi family is head of the tribe, the present representative lives in the Jhelum and receives a pension from Government. In Besa the family of a late Risalhar-Major of the 12th Cavalry is wellknown, and there are other good families in the same village. In Mirpur (Azad Kashmir) there are well-known representatives of the Chibs in Panjeri, Kosgoma, and Lehri.

4. *History and particulars.*—The Chib is a Rajput tribe of high standing. It gave its name to the Chibhal, the hill country of Kashmir on the left bank of the Jhelum river along the Hazara border, though it no longer occupies those hills. The tribe claim descent in the female line from the Katoch and Kangra, and their eponym, Chib Chand, is said to have left Kangra 14 centuries ago and settled near Bhimbar. Sur Sadi was the first of the tribe to become a Muslim, his tomb is still venerated, and no male child is considered a true Chib until his scalp-locks have been offered up at this tomb. Sur Sadi's (or Shadi Khan's) Hindu name was Dharam Chand. He was famed for his skill in medicine and was summoned to Delhi to attend the Emperor Jehangir. He was successful in effecting a cure and received a daughter of the Emperor in marriage, became a Muslim and changed his name to Shadi Khan. He deserted his bride

and fled home, and was eventually killed in an invasion of his country by the Moghals.

The chief of the tribe used to be known as the Raja of Bhimbar.

The tribe is divided into three social grades—Mandial, Garhial, and Dherial, feeling still runs high on the point of these distinctions even though it is difficult to say who is Mandial and who Garhial. The Garhial stand high and will not give their daughters to the others. The Chibs seek marriages for their daughters among Sayads and Gokkhars whom they admit to be their superiors.

There are fourteen septs :—

Rupyal.	Barwana,	Jaskal,
Dhural,	Darwesal,	Malkana.
Mamdal,	Baranshahia,	Ghanlyal and
Samwalia,	Miana,	Ghaghila.
Malkal,	Daphral,	

The tribe is one of short stature, and their men are rather thick set. They are deservedly popular as they make excellent soldiers.

18. Chima.

1. *Population in the Punjab.*—17,600. (census 1931).

2. *Locality.* In the Punjab the tribe is chiefly found in the Sialkot and Gujranwala districts, there are a few also in most of the other Cis-Jhelum districts.

3. *Chief families.*—There is a family of fair status at Badoke, in the Daska tahsil of the Sialkot district.

4. *History and particulars.*—The Chima is one of the largest Jat tribes in the Punjab. It claims descent from the Chauhan Rajput. They fled from Dehli on the defeat of Prithi Raj by Muhammad of Ghor, to Amritsar, where Chotu Mal, a son of Prithi Raj, founded a village on the Beas in the time of Ala-ud-din It is from his grand-son Rana Kang that the Chimas say they are sprung. They are a powerful and united tribe. The bulk of the tribe embraced Islam in the time of Firoze Shah and Aurangzeb, but many retain their old customs. They marry witin the tribe as well with their neighbours.

19. Dhamial.

1. *Population.*—9,500. { (Rajput, 8,000) / (Jat, 1,500). } —(census 1931).

2. *Locality.*—Chiefly found in the Rawalpindi District, but also in Gujrat, Jhelum and Attock.

3. *Particulars.*—The Dhamial are of both Rajput and Jat status. The Rajput branch receive daughters in marriage from the Jat section but do not give girls to them, otherwise the two branches appear to mix freely and are one tribe. They account for themselves as having come originally from Ghazni to the Sialkot district, from whence they went to Dhamiak (Jhelum tahsil) where they built a fort. They take service freely and make satisfactory soldiers.

The Dhamial have no connection with the Dhanials, the two tribes being quite distinct.

20. Dhanial

1. *Male population.*—(Approximately) 3,400. (census 1931).

2. *Locality.*—The Dhanials are found chiefly in the lower spurs of the Murree hills in the Rawalpindi tahsil of the Rawalpindi district; there are about a dozen villages of the tribe in Hazara, and two in Gujar Khan (Rawalpindi).

3. *Chief families.*—The tribe is well represented by pensioned Military Officers in Kala Basand, Dakhian and Karor. The Zaildars of Pind Begwal, Bhambatrar and Chirah are probably the most influential men.

4. *History and particulars.*—The Dhanials claim to be desended from Hazrat Ali, son-in-law of the *Prophet* (Peace be upon him). The Dhanni country in the Chakwal tahsil of Jhelum, is supposed to take its name from the tribe, but no Dhanials are to be found there at the present time and they themselves do not connect themselves with that locality in any way.

The Dhanial must not be confused with the Dhamial who are quite distinct from and have no connection with them. There appears also to be no Jat branch of the tribe, though the census returns have shown a certain number.

The Dhanials inter-marry with the Dhunds, Sattis, Khetwals and Jasgams.

They make good soldiers.

21. Dhudhi.

1. *Population.*—5,800. (census 1931).

2. *Locality.*—This tribe is scattered about Lahore, Shahpur, Jhang, Multan, Sahiwal and the Bahawalpur State.

3. *History.*—This is a small clan of Punwar Rajputs found along the banks of the Sutlej and Chenab. They are supposed to have come originally from Multan. They are said to be "fair agriculturists and respectable members of soceity".

22. Dhund.

1. *Male population.*- { Punjab, 29,000. In Poonch (Azad Kashmir) 7,800. } census of 1931

2. *Locality*—The Dhunds are found chiefly in the Murree tahsil of the Rawalpindi district and the Abbottabad tahsil of Hazara, also on the left bank of the Jhelum in the Bagh tahsil of Poonch.

3. *Chief families.*—The recognised head of the Dhunds belongs to the Phulgraon family in the Rawalpindi tahsil. Other well-known families of the tribe are found at Sehanna, Potha, Dewal, Chattar and Sila in the Rawalpindi district and in Lora, Bakot, Kalahan in Hazara.

4. *History and particulars.*—The Dhunds claim descent from Hazrat Abbas, the paternal uncle of the *Prophet* (Peace be upon him). Another tradition makes Takht Khan who came with Taimur to Delhi, their ancestor. Notwithstanding this claim to purely Muslim ancestry Colonel Wace wrote of the Dhunds than "thirty years ago their acquaintance with the Muslim faith was still slight, and though they now know more of it, and are more careful to observe it, relics of their Hindu faith are still observable in their social habits". It is reported of them that even until recent times they refused to eat with other Muslims or to allow them to

touch their cooking pots. They have now lost this extreme exclusiveness. Among the Punwar clans Tod mentions the Dhoonda and Dhoond which were supposed by him to be extinct, and it is possible that the Dhunds are either one of these.

The tribe was almost exterminated by the Sikhs in 1837.

They are very proud of their tribe.

Physically the Dhunds are a fine race and are intelligent.

The Sattis and the Dhunds are supposed at one time to have been deadly enemies, at the present day the two tribes live amicably together and intermarry freely.

There are four sections of the tribe, which are divided into many "wals" or clans.

1. The Chandal, found chiefly in Poonch in the Bagh tahsil.

2. The Gaiyal, descendants of Gai Khan, whose tomb is near Duberan in the Kahuta tahsil. This section have villages on the right bank of the Jhelum near Tangrot. There is one family in Karor and a few in Poonch.

3. The Ratnial, these are common in the Murree and Abbottabad tahsils.

4. The Andwal, which is a small section in Hazara.

The Jasgams say they are branch of the Dhunds and

though the Dhunds sometimes admit this relationship, it is doubtful whether there is any foundation for it except the mythical descent of both tribes from an uncle and an ancestor of the *Prophet* (peace be upon him).

In the Rawalpindi district the tribe inter-marry with the Sattis, Khetwals, Dhanials and Jasgams. In Hazara with the Karrals.

23. Dogar.

1. *Male population.*—30,000. (census 1931)

2. *Locality.*—This tribe is found in the upper valleys of the Sutlej and Beas rivers above the lower border of the Lahore District; they have also spread westwards along the foot of the hills into the Sialkot district.

3. *History and particulars.*—In social standing the Dogars rank as Rajputs. The trible claim to be of Rajput descent but this is strenuously denied by their Rajput neighbours, and their distinctive physiognomy makes it probable that there is very little Rajput blood in their veins. They are often classed with Gujars, whom they much resemble in their habits.

There are many clans, chief of which are:—

The Matter, China, Tagra, and Chokra.

24. Duli.

1. *Male population.*—1,500. (census 1931)

2. *Locality.*—The Duli are found in the vicinity of Seirha in Mehanda tahsil of Poonch State.

3. *Particulars.*—They claim to be Rajputs and that

the tribe migrated from Jammu. They should make fair soldiers.

25. Gaiyal.

The Gaiyals are a branch of the Dhunds. There are about 200 men serving in the army who belong to this sub-tribe.

26. Gakkhar.

1. *Male population.*—Punjab, 17,200 and Kashmir 6,700 (census 1931)

2. *Locality.*—The Gakkhars are most numerous in the Jhelum tahsil of the Jhelum district. They are found throughout the Rawalpindi district, there is a small section in the Abottabad tahsil of the Hazara district and they are to be met with in Poonch and the Mirpur district of Azad Kashmir. The tribe is heavily recruited in the army.

3. *Chief families.*—The Admal family of Pharwala and the Sarangal family of Khanpur are the best known, the former place is in Rawalpindi and the latter in Hazara. Other well-known representatives are the Sarangal of Saidpur. Admals of Kaniat and Channi in Rawalpindi. In the Jhelum district are the Admals of Sultanpur, the Iskandrials of Lehri and Bakrala and the Bugial families of Domeli, Padri and Baragowah. At Sanghoi, Malhu and Adrana there are also families of good standing.

4. The Gakkhars in popular estimation rank socially above all other Musalman tribes in which they are found, and they refuse to give their daughters in marriage to any but Sayads.

The origin of the tribe is most obscure, and ethnological experts are not agreed as to the race from which they are sprung. Ferishta mentions them as a brave and savage race who lived mostly in the hills and had little or no religion, but the Gakkhars hold that Ferishta has often confused them with the Khokhars, and even that he had a grudge against them for their maltreatment of his ancestor Hindu Shah.

The Gakkhars describe themselves as being descended from Kaigohar, of the Kaiani family once reigning in Isphan that they conquered Kashmir and Tibet and ruled those countries for many generations, but were eventually driven back to Kabul whence they entered the Punjab with Mahmud of Ghaznavi early in the 11th century. This story is rejected by Ibbetson, because it is certain that they held their present possessions long before the Muhammadan invasion of India and also, on Ferishta's showing a Gakkhar army resisted Mahmud and almost turned the tide of victory against him on two occasions.

It is believed however, that the Gakkhars entered India considerably earlier than the date they themselves fix. Some authorities give A. D. 300 as the probable date of their immigration.

The assassination of Shahab-ud-din Ghori has been put down to the Gakkhars, but it seems possible that it was accomplished by the Khokhars with whom the Gakkhars have been confused by Ferishta.

Whatever their origin may be, the history of the Gakkhars, since the first Muslim invasion, is closely interwoven with that of the North West Punjab, and their exploits in the field have always redounded to their credit as fighters.

They were the ruling race in the hill country between the Indus and the Jhelum until the rise of the Sikh power.

Their conversion from nominal Buddhism to Islam, is said to have taken place in 1205 A. D. when they were crushingly defeated by Shahab-ud-din Ghori. At the time of Timur's invasion the Gakkhars were among the foremost of the defenders of India. They also resisted Babar early in the 16th century and were only subdued after a very determined resistance.

Subsequently the Gakkhar chief attended Babar, with a Gakkhar force to Delhi. Under the later Moghals the Gakkhar Rajas governed as feudal chiefs. They espoused the cause of Humayun when be was a fugitive in Afghanistan and it was at this time (1541) that Sher Shah built the famous fort at Rohtas near Jhelum to hold the Gakkhars in check and to hinder Humayun's return. On Humayun's return to power they were richly rewarded for their services and were held in favour by the great Akbar, one of whose most noted generals was a Gakkhar. Their downfall was accomplished by Sardar Gujar Singh, a powerful Sikh chief, who defeated them at Gujrat in 1765; and was further accelerated by internal dissensions.

Their ancient forts are still to be seen at Pharwala, near Kahutah and on the Jhelum at Dangali and Sultanpur.

The Gakkhar chiefs enjoyed the title of Sultan, now

they are known as Raja and sometimes Mirza, though the only family which can rightfully claim the former title is that of the Admal chief of Pharwala.

The Gakkhars, especially those of the Rawalpindi district, are deteriorating physique, owing chiefly to their general indolence, their early marriages and to the prevailing custom of inter-marriage within the clan.

In the Jhelum district they maintain their fine qualities and prosperity.

The Gakkhars are divided into the following branches:—Admal, Sarangal, Firozal, Bugial, Iskandrial, Hatial. Other clans such as the Paharial, Jodhial, Mangral, Kainswal, Farmsial, Sunal, Kul Chandral, Tulial, Sakhal, and Sagial are not recognised as true Gakkhars by the others.

The Gakkhars are deservedly much sought after by both cavalry and infantry regiments for they have on all occasions proved their worth in the field.

It is unlikely that there are as many Gakkhars at the census returns show, or that all those in the army can be members of the tribe.

The Pharwala family and some Sarangals, are said to adhere to Shiah tenets, and some Gakkhars have stated that they were originally all Shiahs. This belief may possibly be attributed to their claim to Persian descent. At the present time none of them can be described as bigoted Shiahs for they do not follow Shiah customs during the Muharram.

27. Gheba.

1. *Male population,*—About 3,800 (census 1931)

2. *Locality.*—The Ghebas are found in the western portion of the Fattehjang tahsil, Attock district.

3. *Chief families.*—The Sardar of Kot is the most important of all the Ghebas. Next are the Malal family. The Dhurnal and Maiyia families are of good standing.

4. *History and particulars.*—The tribe claim to be Moghal and are returned as such in the census reports. The Ghebas have either given their name, or received it, from the Gheb, they explain it as the latter reason and prefer to be known as Moghals. A not improbable conjecture is that they were a small band of broken Rajput families, fleeing from the central Punjab, who joined the Jodhras and settled down on their borders. The tribe rose to independence and in social status in the later years of Sikh rule. They are now considered equal in rank with the Jodhras and Alpials.

The tribe is well off and thrifty.

They are a fine manly race, delighting in hawking and field sports they are horse-breeders and good horsemen.

Owing to their small numbers they can give few men to the army.

28. Ghorewaha.

1. *Male population.*—16,230. (census 1931)

2. *History and particulars.*—The Ghorewaha is of

Rajput descent from Kush, the second son of Rama, Raja Man of Kot Kurman (now Udaipur) had two sons, Kachwaha and Hawah : the tribes state that they are of the lineage of Hawaha. The name Ghorewaha is supposed to be derived from an offering of a horse made by a member of the tribe to Shahab-ud-Din Ghori. The tribe settled in its present tract while it was still Hindu, and in the time of Akbar their possession would seem to have been more extensive than they are now.

They are said to give their daughters to the Naru Rajputs. Their physique is good, especially in the village near the foot of the hills and they are anxious for military service.

The tribe sends many emigrants to foreign countries, especially to Australia, Africa and the United States of America.

29. Gondal.

1. *Male population.*—19,000. (census 1931)

2. *Locality.*—The Gondals are found chiefly in the Bhera tahsil of the Shahpur district in the tract known as the Gondal Bar. They are also found in the Gujarat, Jhelum and Rawalpindi districts. Those in Jhelum and Rawalpindi have no connection with the true Gondals of the Bhera, and are unlike them in general appearance and in their characteristics.

4. *Chief Families.*—There are some families of special importance. The Zaildars of Miani Gondal and Kot Moman are men of influence.

5. *History and particulars.*—The Gondal's claim to be Chauhán Rajputs and say that their ancestor came from Naushahra in the south to Pakpattan where he was converted to Islam by Bawa Farid (رحمتہ اللہ علیہ), if this is so they probably occupied their present abodes within the last six centuries. The tribe now ranks as Jat, it intermarriages freely with the other Jat tribes of the districts, such as the Ranjhas, the Harrals and Laks. Formerly, before the Jhelum canal was introduced into their country, they were a pastoral people subsisting almost entirely on the produce of their large herds of cattle. Now they are, taking more and more to agriculture and are in very easy circumstances. Physically they are a fine race, strong and well made.

The Gondals are well fitted for military service.

30. Gujars.

1. *Male population.*—2, 83, 495 (census 1931)

2. *Locality.*—The Gujars are distributed throughout the Punjab and Hazara.

3. *History and Particulars.*—The history of this people has been given in Chapter 1.

Gujar clans are most numerous, the following being the best known and most suitable for military service:—

Kathana . . . 51,000	Cheschi . . . 39,000
Chaudam . . . 27,000	Kasana . . . 15,000

Poswal ... 28,000	Bhamla ... 4,000
Kalas ... 12,000	Bijar ... 19,000
Monan ... 9,000	Gorsi ... 19,000
Thakria ... 9,000	

All these, with the exception of the Poswal, claim Rajput descent from some one of the best known Rajput tribes. The Poswal say they came into India with Wajih Kalbi, a companion of the *Prophet* ﷺ (peace be upon him) who accompanied Ahutas ruler of Yemen when he conquered Kashmir, and they subsequently settled in the Sialkot district. At the present time this clan is indistinguishable from other Gujars and has the same customs and ceremonials.

No one of these clans can claim any definite superiority over the rest, but some are more exclusive than the others as to whom they give their daughters in marriage. The Kathana, for example, used to consider it derogatory to give daughters to any Gujar at all and sought bridegrooms in more exalted families.

Gujars rank in most districts with Jats and Ahirs.

Gujars vary greatly with the locality in which they are found, those in the hills quite unlike the caste of the same designation in the plains. In the hills they are exclusively pastoral, they cultivate scarcely at all and maintain their existence by the sale of the produce of their herds. In the plains they are generally good cultivators but, there also, always keep cattle or sheep and goats.

31. Harral.

1. *Male population.*—(Approximately) 5,000. (census 1931)

2. *Locality.*—The Harral are found in the Sahiwal Jhang and Shahpur districts.

3. The Harral are a Jat clan of unknown origin.

32. Hoon or Hun.

1. *Population.*—Under 500 (census 1931).

2. *Locality.*—The Hun are located chiefly in the Rawalpindi tahsil of the Rawalpindi district, there are also a few in the Gujar Khan tahsil and some in Hazara.

Headmen.—The Zaildar of Gujar Khan belongs to this clan.

4. *Particulars.*—The Hun are Panwar Rajputs descended from a Raja Judgeo. The tribe is a very small one.

33. Jalap.

1. *Male population.*—400 (census 1931)

2. *Locality.*—This small tribe is met with chiefly in the Pind-Dadun Khan tahsil of the Jhelum district, there are also a few small villages in the Bhera tahsil of Shahpur.

3. *Chief families.*—The best known families reside at Chak Sadi and Pinnanwal.

4. *History and particulars.*—The Jalaps claim to be Khokhar Rajputs, but their neighbours do not admit this

claim. They rank with Lillas and Phaphras and are probably below Rajput status, but considerably above that of Jat.

The tribe is well off and have not taken to military service until lately. It is certain that without fighting qualities they could not have maintained themselves in the most valuable tract in the Jhelum district, against the Janjuas and others.

34 Janjua.

1. *Male population.*—Approximately 12,000 (census 1931).

2. *Locality.*—The Janjuas are most numerous in the Pind-Dadun-Khan and Jhelum tahsils of the Jhelum district; there is also a large branch of the tribe in the Kahuta tahsil of Rawalpindi. They are found in small numbers scattered about the Punjab and North-West of Frontier. In the Shahpur district there are two villages owned by a branch of the tribe which appears to be quite distinct from the others.

The tribe is heavily recruited in the army; over twenty Infantry and several Cavalry Regiments enlist them.

3. *Chief families.*—The Darapur family is, perhaps, the best known, it has given many Officers to the Army: In Chakri Malot, Saloi, Walwal and Wahali, all of which are in the Jhelum district, good representatives of the Janjuas are to be found. In Kahuta is the Mator family, and in Shahpur one of good status in Khutta Sagral.

4. *History and particular.*—The Janjuas are said to be of Rajput descent. According to Mr. Thomson:—"At

some uncertain period, some clans of Rahthor Rajputs, emigrating from Jodhpur, occupied the uplands of the Salt Range. The leader of this movement, according to common account, was Raja Mal. The Rajputs first seated themselves at Malot in the west Salt Range. If Babar be read with attention it will be seen that he represents the Janjuas as confined to the hills, and ruling over various subject tribes, who cultivated the plains. The Janjuas were long the predominant race in the centre and west of the district (Jhelum). When Sultan Mahmud of Ghazni invaded India the Janjuas opposed him, were defeated, and fled to the jungles. Mahmud followed them up and succeeded in capturing Raja Mal himself. The Raja was released on condition that he and his tribe should embrace Islam. When the conversion took place the 'janju' or caste thread was broken, and the neophytes have been called Janjuas ever since."

It is impossible that the Raja Mal who led the tribe from Jodhpur to the Salt Range, was the same person who was captured by Mahmud. The first event must have preceded the second by some centuries, and another account which relates that Jaipal, who opposed Mahmud at Nandana 900 years ago, is their ancestor, is probably more correct. "Raja Mal is a little mythical and any action of doubtful origin is apt to be fathered upon him."

The tribe was well established between Nilab and Bhera when Babar visited the country.

They were the natural enemies of the Gakkhars from time immemorial.

Raja Mal had six sons:—

Raja Wir and Jodh, whose descendants are found in the Jhelum district. Those of Jodh being also found in the Kharian tahsil of Gujrat.

Kakha—whose descendants are found in Poonch and Kashmir, and are known as Kakkhe.

Tarnoli—from whom spring the Tanaolis of Hazara (the Tanaolis do not agree to this and claim Moghal origin).

Dabuchara—descendants found in Hazara (and known as Janjuas) and also in Sialkot.

Pir Kala—the Kahrwal and Dallal Janjuas of the Kahro ilaqua of Rawalpindi (Kahuta tahsil) are the descendants of this son.

With the exception of the descendants of Wir and Jodh the others are now distinct tribes, having nothing in common and not even inter-marrying. The Janjuas of the Salt Range are the most aristocratic and make the best soldiers.

The Janjuas were, at the time of Babar's visit (1526 A.D.) the predominant race in the Salt Range. They subsequently became divided, lost their strength in combination, and the Awans and Gakkhars were able to contend successfully against them and wrest much of their power and territory from them. When the Sikh power arose, the Janjuas like the Gakkhars and Awans, came under their rule, not however, without much stubborn resistance. They held out for many months, in their strongholds at Makhiala and Kusak, but were eventually compelled to capitulate from the want of water. Raujit Singh himself is said to have undertaken the siege operations against Kusal. The Sikhs took over the salt mines at Khewra which had been their most valued possession.

The Janjuas rank second only to the Gakkhars in the Jhelum and Rawalpindi districts. Their headmen are known as Sultan and the second son as Malik. In the Jhelum district the tribe is invariably known as "raja," the word Janjua hardly ever being heard.

Janjua goots are found among such menials as Telis, Lohars, Tarkhans and Musallis.

Their observances at various ceremonials are much the same as those of the Chibs.

The Janjuas are said to be the only really pure Rajputs in the plains of the Punjab. They have great pride of race (as being Janjuas) and make fine soldiers, most suitable for cavalry, as they are of light build.

35. Jaral.

1. *Male population.*—4,000. (census 1931)

2. *Lacality.*—The Jaral are found in the Riasi and Mirpur districts of Kashmir.

3. *Particulars.*—The Jarals are Rajputs of good standing. They are said to have given Raja Gulab Singh much trouble. The rank above the Mangrals and intermarry with no other tribe, but give their daughters to Gakkhars.

36. Jasgam.

1. *Male population.*—The Jasgams have been included among the Dhunds in the last census. They number probably about 1,200 males. (census 1931).

2. *Locality*—This tribe is found near Panjar in the Kahuta tahsil (Rawalpindi).

Headmen.—A family which was rewarded for its services in 1857 in Salitta is head of the clan.

5. *History and particulars.*—The Jasgams, like the Dhunds and Khatrils, claim descent from Manaf an ancestor of the *Prophet* ﷺ (peace be upon him) and they say that they got possession of the tract they now occupy under Gakkhar rule, when one Hazrat Zubair, a descendant of the *Prophet*, (peace be upon him) came from Arabia and settled near Kahuta. On this claim they represent themselves as Dhunds and wish to be enlisted as such. They did not join the Dhunds in their attempted raid on Murree in 1857 and in character they more resemble the Sattis. They intermarry freely both with the Sattis and Dhunds.

The tribe is a very small one and not very prosperous They accept all the military service they can get and make satisfactory soldiers.

The Khatril are found in small numbers in Gujar Khan and Mandra and are classed as Rajputs.

37. Jat.

Besides the Punjabi Musalman Jat tribes described in this chapter, there are innumerable divisions and subdivisions of Jats throughout the Punjab; a description of each will be found in "a glossary of the tribes and castes of the Punjab and North-West Frontier Province, 1911.

The census report of 1931 gives the male population as 16,04,628.

38. Jatal.

1. *Male population.* — About 750 (census 1931)

2. *Locality* — The Jatal are found in Kahuta Tahsil of Rawalpindi district.

3. *Particulars.* — They are classed as Rajputs. They make good soldiers.

39. Jethal.

1. *Male population* — About 500 (census 1931)

2. *Lolality.* — The Jethal are found in the Jhelum thal between the Jhelum river and the Lilla estate.

Particulars — They claim Bhatti Rajput descent, but other people say they are Bhuttas and in this they are supported by their pedigree table. They make good soldiers.

40. Jodhra.

1. *Male population.* — Approximately 1,400. (Census 1931).

2. *Lacality.* — The Jodhras inhabit the south-eastern portion of the Pindigheb tahsil and the valley of the Sohan extending, on the south, to the Talagang border.

3. *Chief families.* — The Maliks of Pindigheb, who are closely related by marriage with the Gheba family of Kot, have great possessions and are the best known.

4. *History and particulars.*—The Jodhras account for themselves as being of Rajput origin, and derive their name from Jodhra who was converted to Islam by Mahmud of Ghazni, and who settled in Kashmiir.

They appear, however, to have come to the Attock district about the end of the 16th century as a small band of military adventurers. They possessed themselves of the Sohan and Sill " illaquas " and much of Talagang. The Awans, the original owners, were not evicted but remained as tenants under the conquering Jodhras, who never themselves cultivated.

The Jodhras became independent chiefs keeping up a large body of armed retainers. Their power was recognised by the Moghals, and Malik Aulia Khan, their first chief known to history, held a revenue assignment of Pindigheb, Talagang and parts of Chakwal.

Owing to family feuds and other causes the tribe has lost much of its original prosperity and is now much less well-to-do than its neighbours, the Ghebas, who have been their ancient rivals and enemies. The two tribes now inter-marry and are on friendly terms.

The Jodhras breed horses and are fond hawking and field sports. They prefer service in Cavalry to Infantry, and being usually of light build are more suitable to that arm.

40. Joiya.

1. *Population.*—37,190 (Census 1931).

2. *Locality.*—The Joiya are found on both banks of the Sutlej from the Multan-Montgomery boundary to

nearly as far down as its confluence with the Indus. Also in Lahore, Multan and Muzaffargarh, and Shahpur. They are numerous in Bahawalpur.

3. *Chief families.*—The Joiyas as a tribe regard the Rais of Shahr Farid as their chief, and his influence extends over the Joiyas of Multan. No Joiya who has committed a fault will deny the fact in the presence of his chief.

4. *History and particulars.*—The Joiya is one of the 36 Royal races of Rajputs, but at the present time at least one-third of their number is returned as Jat. The ancient chronicles describe them as holding Hariana, Bhatiana Bhatner and Nagor, and also in common with the Dehia, with whom their name is always coupled, the banks of the Indus and Sutlej near their confluence.

Some seven centuries ago they were apparently driven out of the Indus tract and partly subjugated by the Bhattis. In Bahawalpur the Daudpotras overcame them in the time of Nadir Shah.

In Sahiwal and Multan the Joiyas as a tribe appear to rank both as Jats and Rajputs, and in Shahpur as Jats.

They are considered a brave race. They are devoted to horses and buffaloes.

The Joiya septs are very numerous. The Lakhwera clan is the highest in the social scale and has a grat reputation for courage. The men are generally short and of light physique.

42. Junhal

1. *Male population.*—About 700. (Census 1931)

2. *Localty.*—The Juhnal are found in Poonch State and also Kahuta Tehsil of Rawalpindi District.

3. *Particulars.*—The Junhal claim to be Rajputs.

They were once numerous and powerful but were nearly all destroyed by the Gakkhars. They make good soldiers.

43. Kahlon

1. *Male population.*—13,000. (Census 1931).

2. *Lacality.*—The bulk of the tribe is found in the Zafarwal tahsil of the Sialkot district ; it is also numerous in the Gujranwala district.

3. *Headmen.*—The most important representative of tribe in the Sialkot district is the Zaildar of Dullan in the Zafarwal tahsil.

History and particulars.—The Kahlon rank as Jat, and claim descent from Raja Vikramajit of the lunar race, through Raja Jagdeo of Daranagar, concerning whom they tell the well worn legend that in his generosity he promised his sister whatsoever she might ask. She claimed his head and he fulfilled his promise, but was miraculously restored to life. His descendant in the 4th generation, Kahlwan gave his name to the tribe. Fourth from him came Soli or Sodi under whom they left Daranagar and settled near Batala in Gurdasaur, whence they spread to Sialkot.

The Muslim portion of the tribe appear to have been converted to Islam, not much time passed.

The tribe is agricultural and the men of good physique.

They inter-marry with Jats of good standing.

44. Kahlotra

The Kahlotra is a small tribe of fair social standing found in the south eastern portion of the Kotli tahsil of Poonch. (Azad Kashmir)

45. Kahrwal.

Male population.—Approximately 1,600. (Census 1931).

2.—*Locality.*—The Kahrwal are found in the Kahuta tahsil of the Rawalpindi district.

3. *Chief families.*—There are no families of much importance, but those of Dulal and Mator are probably the best known. The Zaildar of Kahuta belongs to the Dula sept.

4. *History and particulars.* - The Kahrwal is a branch of the Janjuas of the Salt Range, their social position being somewhat below that section of the tribe.

They rank above the ordinary Rajput and are a fine, sturdy, self-respecting race. They are far from prosperous, and even in their richest villages, are largely dependent on military service. A large number have become Military Officers.

They claim descent from Pir Kala, a son of Raja Mal, who married Kaho Rani when he came to the Kahuta hills, and named the ilaqua Kahru after her. Hence the descendants are called Kahrwal.

The Dulal is a sub-division of the tribe. This branch should not be confused with the Dolal Qureshis of Gujar Khan.

46. Kahut

1. *Male population.* —5,500. (Census 1931).

2. *Locality.* —The bulk of tribe is in the Chakwal tahsil of the Jhelum district, small numbers are found scatterd about the Rawalpindi, Hazara, Gujart and Shahpur districts.

3. *Chief families.* —The best known are in Kariala (Jhelum). In Langah and Ramshinh are also representative families.

4. *History and particu'ars.* —The Kahut claim to have come from Arabia and to be of *Koreshi* origin, but this is not acknowledged by others. It seems unlikely that they are of Rajput extraction.

The Kahuta hills of the Rawalpindi district are supposed to have derived their name from the tribe, but no record remains of them in that tract.

About the year A. D. 1359 their ancestor Said Nawab Ali migrated to Delhi, on the way he defeated a pagan king of Sialkot, named Sain Pal. On reaching Delhi they paid there respects to the King who ordered to hold the Dhanni (in Chakwal) and the Salt Range on his behalf. They accordingly retraced their steps and settled at the foot of the Salt Range, realising the revenue from the Janjuas and the Gujar graziers and remitting it to Delhi. Chaudri Sahnsar, 8th in descent from Kahot, was their ancestor in the time of Babar.

They may be considered to rank as Rajputs in social status.

The Kahuts inter-marry to some extent with the Mairs and Kassars and now and then with Awans, both giving and taking daughters.

They have no special customs except that the males will not wear blue clothes, or if they do they fall ill !

They are bold man of independent character, and of good physique, keen sportsmen and good riders.

The tribe has no clans.

47. Kakkezai.

1. *Male population (in the Punjab).* 8,400. (Census 1931).

2. *Locality.*—The Kakkezai are scattered about the Punjab, the most numerous clans being in Lahore and Sialkot.

3. *Leading families.*—Probably the best known in the Pasrur family in the Sialkot district.

4. *History and particulars.*—The Kakkezai claim to be of Pathan extraction, descended from Afghans of Sistan. They are known as Sheikhs. It is probable that they, like the Khoja Hindus, were converted at an early period of the Muslim invasions and affiliated to a Pathan class. Sir Denzil Ibbetson says of them " the class (Kalal) was raised in importance, many of its members abandoned there hereditary occupation (of distilling liquor) and its Musalman section also grew ashamed of the social stigma conveyed by the confession of Kalal origin, it occordingly

fabricated a story of Pathan origin, and adding to the first letter of the caste name the Pathan tribal termination called itself Kakkezai. The name was at first only used by the most wealthy members of the caste, but its use is spreading. The well-known sheikhs are Kalals, who while claiming Pathan origin call themselves Sheikhs. They are now mostly known as Muslim traders and are found all over Pakistan and as far west as Kandahar. They as clever and usually prosperous, generally arriving at distinction where employed, and most anxious for aristocratic status.

48. Kakkhe.

1. *Male population.*—Approximately 1,500. (Census 1931).

Locality.—This tribe is found on the left bank of the Jhelum between Kohala and Uri (Kashmir), and also in the Bagh tahsil of Poonch.

3. *Particulars.*—The Kakkhe claim to be of Rajput descent from Kakha, a son of Raja Mal, the ancestor of the Janjuas. They share with Bambas, a privileged status in the Jhelum valley, both are styled Raja and both are looked on as the most aristocratic of the Jhelum tribes. They inter-marry only with each other.

The Kakkhes and Bambas successfully resisted Akbar's first invasion of Kashmir and drove him back in 1582. Under the Afghans they were practically independent.

The Kakkhe appear to hava fallen somewhat from their former high estate, but they are still a well-made handsome race, and should make efficient soldiers

The Tezal are sub-division of the Kakkhe.

49. Kambohs.

1. *Male population.*—54,481. (Census 1931).

2. *Locality.*—The Kambohs are found in the upper Sutlej valley as low down as Sahiwal.

3. *History and particulars.*—The Kambohs are commonly supposed to be closely related to the Arains. Sir Denzil Ibbetson and other authorities, however, consider it doubtful if this supposed relationship has any further basis than the fact that Kambohs and Arains both came from the west, and are both of much the same social and agricultural repute. The Kambohs are not merely agriculturists, as they infrequently engage in trade, and have even taken service in the Army, in offices, and as private servants.

They claim Rajput descent from Raja Karan.

Musalman Kambohs held Sohna, in Gurgaon, some centuries ago and the tombs and mosques left by them show that they must have injoyed a considerable position. Several Kamboh Sardars were Amirs and Mansabdars in the Court of Akbar, and one of the Emperor's generals, Shahbaz Khan, who greatly distinguished himself in Rengol, was a members of this tribe.

In appearance the Mussalman Kambohs are generally of short stature, their physical development is good and their intelligence appears to be up to the average.

50. Karral.

1. *Male population.*—11,300. (Census 1931)

2. *Locality.*—The Karrals are found on the right bank of the Harro river in the Nara tract, between the Rajoia plain and the Dunga Gali range in the Hazara district, and also in the Boi hills of the same district.

3. *Leading families.*—The Jagirdars of Diwal Manal and Dabran.

4. *History and particulars.*—The Karrals are believed to be Indians in origin, though they themselves deny it, and claim to be Moghals, who came from Kian. Their ancestor, Kallar Shah was, they say, in the service of an Emperor of Delhi, with whom he went to Kashmir. On his return he took the Bakot tract and Nara hills from the Gakkhars. As a matter of fact, it is more probable that the Karrals were already in these parts when the Gakkhars invaded their country. They appear to have thrown off the Gakkhar yoke in the 17th century.

The ordinary members of the tribe seem to be in very poor circumstances and their Physique is not good.

They inter-marry with the Dhunds of Hazara, with whom they are supposed, by some to be identical in origin.

51. Kashmiri.

Male population.—1,13,759. (Census 1931).

Lahore Division	75,298
Rawalpindi Division	32,875
Multan Division	3,603
Punjab States	1,983
Total	113,759

The word Kashmiri is perhaps, applicable to the members of any of the races of Kashmir, but it is commonly used in Kashimir itself to denote the people of the valley of Srinagar. In any case the term is a geographical one, and probably includes many of what we should, in the Punjab, call separate castes. In the Punjab the term Kashmiri connotes a Musalman Kashmiri. Most immigrants from Kashmir are called Kashmiris whatever their original tribe. These must be distinguished from the well-known Musalman tribes of Poonch and Jammu who are mostly of Rajput descent and not Kashmiris at all. The Kashmiris are a prosperous class and seek eagerly for military employment, many have risen to commissioned rank. The principal tribes in the Punjab are Bat, Batte, Dar, Lun, Mahr, Man, Mir, Shaikh, Wain and Warde.

52. Kassar (Moghal.)

1. *Male population.* —Approximately 4,000. (Census 1931).

2. *Locality.*—The Kassars are peculiar to the north west quarter of the Chakwal tahsil, Jhelum district.

2. *Chief families.*—The best known family is that of Dullah the head of which is the Zaildar. Another family of good standing is the one at Chawli, a member of which received a direct commission in an Infantry Regiment.

3. *History and particulars*—The Kassars were noted at one time for claiming neither Rajput, Awan or Moghal origin, they asserted that they came originally from Jammu and that they obtained their present territories by

joining the armies of Babar. Since the census of 1881 they have recorded themselves as Moghals, and this claim have now developed into a genealogical tree in which the Kassars are shown as being of common origin with the Moghal Emperors. They now account for themselves as follows :—

They were originally located in the country of Kinan in Asia Minor, whence they migrated to Ghazni at some time unknown, with the ancestor of the Moghal dynasty, and subsequently accompanied Babar in his invasion of India in A. D. 1526. Their ancestors at that time being Gharka and Bhin according to same, or Jhajha, Lati and Kaulshinh according to others. All agree however, in stating that Gharka is buried on a mound in Mauza Hatar not many miles from Dhok Pipil in Bal Kassar which is said to be the original settlement of the tribe in these parts. The Dhanni was then in the hands of wandering Gujars, while Changas Khan Janjua held the hills to the south living at fort Samarkand in Mauza Maira. Babar made over to them the western portion of the Dhanni, on condition that the would drain off the water with which the eastern part was then covered, and Gharka obtained some additional country to the south-west as a reward for restoring to Changas Khan a favouritemare, which the Janjua raja had lost.

They state that the original profession of the tribe was "hakumat" or government, and that it is now agriculture or Government employment.

Their headmen receive the tittle of "Chaudhri."

Their customs do not differ from the tribes surrounding them. They hold a good position among the tribes of the Jhelum district, ranking in popular estimation with the Mairs and Kahuts. They inter-marry freely with the former, both giving and taking daughters, but a Kassar of good family who married his daughter to a Kahut of fair standing, incurred the displeasure of the brother-hood. They do not inter-marry with any other tribe.

In character the Kassar is supposed to be passionate and revengeful, given to bitter feuds—which may be said to be a common trait in these parts.

Their Chaudris are men of engaging manners and fine appearance, good riders and fond of hawking. They breed a very fair stamp of horse.

Their average physique is good and they should prove excellent material for the army.

53. Kathia.

1. *Male population.*—1,600. (Census 1931).

2. *Locality.*—The Kathias are found in the Ravi valley of the Multan and Sahiwal districts, also in the south of the Jhang district.

3. *History and particulars.*—The Kathias claim to be Punwar Rajputs descended from a Rajput prince named Kathia who lived about the time of their conversion to Islam, in the reign of the Emperor Akbar. An attempt has been made to identify the tribe with the Kathoei, who in their stronghold at Sangla, so stoutly resisted the victorious army of Alexandar, but it cannot be said that anything definite is known about the tribe.

They are of Jat status.

Their average physique is good, owing to the fact that they do not allow their children of either sex to marry until they have attained the age of puberty.

64. Kethwal.

1. *Male population.*—1,250 (Census 1931).

2. *Locality.*—The Charihan spur of the Murree range is the home of the Kethwalas, this tract is in the Murree tahsil of the Rawalpindi district.

3. *Headmen.*—There are no families of importance, the Zaildar of Chirihan and some Military Officers form the aristocracy of the tribe.

4. *History and particulars.* The Kethwal belong to the same group as the Dhund and Satti, but claim decent from Alexander the Great !

They say that they are the oldest inhabitants of these hills and that they came into them before either the Dhund or Satti. They were almost exterminated by the Dhunds, at some time, the date of which is uncertain and they are now a very small tribe. Their appearance and character much resumble that of the Dhunds, but their physique is not so good. The tribe is a poor one and is glad to accept all the military employment it can secure. The Kethwals inter-marry with the Dhund, Satti and Dhandial.

55. Khakha.

1. *Population.*—11,260. (Census 1931).

2. *Locality.*— The tribe is to be met with practically throughout the Punjab.

3. *Particulars.*—The Khakhas are supposed to be Khatris converted to Islam. They engage exclusively in trade.

56. Kharral.

1. *Male population.*—18,650. (Census 1931).

2. *Locality.*—The Kharrals are common in the Sahiwal district and are also found in Lahore, Gujranwala, Multan and Bahawalpur. The valley of the Ravi, from the junction with the Chenab to the boundary between Lahore and Sahiwal is the chief habitat of this tribe.

3. *Chief families.*—The best known and one of most importance is the Kamalia talukdar family which is mentioned in "Punjab Chiefs".

4. *History and particulars.*—The Kharrals appear to be a true Rajput tribe, though a considerable portion of them are styled Jat. They trace their origin from one Bhupa, a descendant of Raja Karan who settled at Uchh and was there converted to Islam. From Uchh they moved to their present territory. They are now divided into two main factions, the upper Ravi and the lower Ravi, the headquarters of the latter being at Ket Kamalia.

The Kamalia Kharrals rose to some prominace in the time of Alamgir, but the upper Kharrals are now the more powerful. They stoutly resisted the English Army in 1857.

Their physique is above the average, and their activity and endurance is remarkable. The tribe has been chiefly a pastoral one.

Many of them served in Ranjit Singh's army.

57. Khattar.

1. *Male population.*—7,730. (Census 1931)

9. The Khattar country is the Kala Chitta range of the Attock district and extends from Hassan Abdal and Jani-ki-Sang to the Indus. There are also a few villages near Shah-ki-Dehri in the Rawalpindi district.

3. —*Chief families.*—The best known families are those of Wah and Dhreik both of which are mentioned in Sir Lepel Griffin's "Punjab Chiefs." The Dhreik family has suffered much from internal feuds, ruinous litigation and bad conduct. The Bahtar branch of this family is of considerable importance.

4. *History and particulars.*—Socially the Khattars hold an intermediate place, ranking below the Awans, Ghebas, Jodhras and other high class Rajputs.

The Khattars themselves are divided in belief as to their descent, while some claim Indian origin, others deny it and allege that they are closely allied to the Awans, having come from Arabia. The Awans do not always admit this relationship.

The Khattars were some time divided into two main branches, though they themselves rarely speak of it. These are the Kala Khattars and Chitta Khattars. To the former belongs the Dhreik family, to the latter the Wah family. The Kala branch, who are darkish in colour, are converted Hindus, and the Chitta of true Musalman descent overpowering and observing their predecessors.

Sir Lepel Griffin makes them originally inhabitants of Khorasan, who come to India with the early Musalman invaders.

The Khattars are now anxious for military sevice, preferring cavalry.

They used to have a name for keeping horses and hawks, but their circumstances in the present day do not appear to permit of much expenditure in this direction.

There are numerous sects though they are not often mentioned. The chief being : —

> Firozal, Sarhal, Isal, Garhal, Balwal, Mitha, Kharial, Jandal, and Ranial.
>
> They give their daughters, to Gakkhars, Awans, Pathans, and Sayads, but receive them only from Awans.

58. Khokhar

1. *Male population.*—32,6,00. (Of which 12,000 are Jats). (Census 1931).

Locality.—The Khokhars are found throughout the Punjab, but chiefly in the Shahpur, Jhang, Multan districts and in the Chenab Colony and Bahawalpur State.

3. *Chief families.*—The Khokhars, are well presented by families of good standing, some of the best known are :—

> In Shahpur, the Malakwal family in the Bhera, tahsil, others in Majoka Jaura, and Bandiol in the Khushab tahsil, and also the Barath family near Miani Gondal.

In the Jhelum district are the Pind-Dadan-Khan and Ahmedabad families and of Badshah Khan in the Chakwal tahsil.

In the Gujrat district the Garhi Gauhar Khan family of the Phalian tahsil.

5. *History and particulars.*—Rajputs, Awans, Jats, and Arains, have all Khokhars branch and the Khokhars themselves vary in status.

The origin of the Khokhars is as obscure as that of any Punjab tribe. Tradition invariably connects them with the Awans, making Khokhar one of Qutab Shah's sons and Khokhar Qutb Shahis his descendants, who would thus be akin to the Juhans, an Awan tribe in the Sialkot. But this pedigree probably mainly records the fact that the Awans and Khokhars owe their conversion to Islam to Saints Qutbshah or his disciples, or that they both accepted his teachings.

In Sialkot Khokhars inter-marry with other tribes which the Awans will not do. In Gujrat, where they hold a compact block of village about Mung on the Jhelum, the leading Khokhars are called Raja, as being of Rajput decent. Yet they claim kinship with the Awans and inter-marry with them and the Bhattis, giving wives to Chibs but not getting brides in return.

About Pind-Dadan-Khan the Rajput Khokhars are said to be entirely distinct from the Jat Khokhars, though elsewhere in the Jhelum district the tribe has become merged with the Jat cultivators. Those of Rajputs status marry into some of the best Janjua families.

The Khokhars have at times been confused with the Gakhars, who state that the historian Ferishta has himself made this mistake. The Khokhars were well settled in the Punjab centuries before the Gakkhars, and were early spread all over the central districts of the province before the Gakkhars acquired their seats in the Salt Range and in the hilly country extending from the Jhelum to the Khanpur "ilaqa" in Hazara, to which they have always been confined.

The earliest distinct mention of the Khokhars occurs in the "Taj-ul-Ma'asir," a History written in A.D. 1905, which describes a revolt of the tribe against Sultan Muhammad of Ghor in the country between the Jhelum and the Chenab, when they were defeated by Qutb-ud-Din Aibak. After this the tribe is repeatedly mentioned in Islamic historical records as breaking out into rebellion and giving trouble generally. The localities with which they are identified were Lahore, the Salt Range, Multan, between the Indus and the Chenab and also east of the Beas river. They appear to have played an important part in the resistance offered to the invading armies of Timur. Sheikh Kukari, one of their leaders, submitted to Timur and was employed by him in his advance on Delhi. After Shaika, Jasrath makes his appearance, in A. D. 1420 he attacked the King of Kashmir who was marching into Sindh, captured him and took all his "material". Jasrath appears to have harried the country with varying success (attacking Lahore itself on two occasions until 1432, when he disappears. In the time of Akbar the Khokhars held portions of the Bari Doab, the Jullunder and Rachna Doabs, Multan and portions of Jammu and Sialkot, with a population estimated at 200,000 souls. Prior to the historical records of the tribe a traditional history of the Khokhars commences their record from about 1500 B. C. and makes them Descendants of Bustam Raja surnamed Kokra, who was governor of the Punjab. Driven thence by Faridur who had acquired the Persian throne, Bustan sought refuge in the hill of Ghor, West of Kandahar, where his people ruled for generations, being called Ghori of Ghoria. Later the Khokhars re-entered the Punjab under chiefs such as Jot, Sirkap, Vikram and many others, and thenceforth held the Punjab.

The Jhelum, Gujrat and Shahpur districts produce the best men.

59. Kichi and Khilchi.

1. *Population*—5,000. (Census 1931)

2. *Locality.*—The Kichi are found almost exclusively round Mailsi in the Multan district, and in the Gugera tahsil of Montgomery.

3. *History and particulars.*—The Kichi is a tribe of Jat status which claims Chauhan (Rajput) origin and descent, from one Kichi, a ruler in Ajmer. Driven out of Delhi by the Muhammadans his descendants migrated to Multan. The tribe fought with the Joiyas, then paramount in those parts, and they say also that they were sent against the rebellious Baluch of Khai by the Moghals, in Multan. In Montgomery they state that they were converted to Islam by Bahawal Haqq.

There is a Jat tribe in Shahpur named Khilchi who have probably originated from the Khilji, a Moghal sub-tribe.

60. Kizilbash.

1. *Population.*—220. (Census 1931)

2. *Locality.*—This very small clan is found cheifly in the Lahore and Lyallpur districts.

Several prominent members of the tribe are serving as Officers in the Army as well as in the civil.

3. *Leading families.*—The best known family is that of Nawab Muzaffar Ali Khan of Lahore. In the Dehra Ismail Khan district there are also families of good status.

4. *History and particulars.*—The original Kizilbash were a tribe of Tartar horsemen from the Eastern Caucasus, who formed the backbone of the old Persian army and of the force with which Nadir Shah invaded India. Many of the great Moghal ministers have been Kizilbash, and notably Mir Jumla, the famous minister of Aurangzeb.

They form an important military colony in Kabul. Those found in the Punjab are descendants of the families who came with Nadir Shah or after him.

They are all Shiahs.

61. Koreshi

1. *Male population (in the Punjab).*—Over 50,000. (Census 1931). It is probable how-ever, that comparatively few of those who have returned themselves as Koresh have any real title to the name.

2. *Locality.*—Koreshis are found throughout the Punjab, they are most numerous in the Rawalpindi, Multan and Jhang districts.

3. *Leading families.*—In the Gujar Khan tahsil (Rawalpindi) is the family of a pensioned Subedar Major

who was A.D.C. to the Commander-in-Chief and a Zaildar. The family of the Ilaqadar of Banhar, Chak Misri, Pindi-Dadun-Khan tahsil (Jhelum). In the Shorkot tahsil of Jhang there are several families, known as Sheikhs, here a title of honour. The "Makhdum" family of Multan and other well-known Koreshi families in the Multan district, two of whom are descendants of the Saint Bahawal Haqq.

4, *History and particulars.*—The Koreshis claim descent form the tribe to which the *Prophet* ﷺ (peace be upon him) belonged. Among those who so style themselves many claim to belong to the Faruqis or descendants of Hazrat Umar, the second Kaliph, or to Sadiqis or descendants of Hazrat Abu Bakar the first Kaliph both of whom were Koreshi by tribe.

In Gujar Khan there is a well-known section known as Dolal, among whom there have been several distinguished Officers.

Another section in the same tahsil is known as Jagial.

The Shorkot Koreshis (Jhang district) have an excellent record as soldiers.

The tribe is respected by for its sanctity.

The best class are agriculturists.

62. Lillas.

1. *Male population.*—890. (Census) (1931)

2. *Locality.*—This small tribe is peculiar to the Jhelum district and lives west of, and near to, Pind-Dadun Khan.

3. *Headmen.*—The Lumbardars of their four villages :—Lilla Bharwana, Lilla Hindwana, Lilla Bhera and Lilla Guj.

4. *History and particulars.*—The Lillas wish to be known as Moghals, but are of Jat rank. They state that they are relations of the Prophet ﷺ (peace be upon him) on his mother's side, and therefore if they had their rights, are Koreshis.

In the time of Sultan Mahmud of Ghazni, a member of the tribe migrated to India with a band of 160 men as as well dependants. After many wanderings from Multan to Gujranwala they finally settled in their present home.

They are Sunni Muslims and say they were so long before their migration to India. They show no signs of Indian origin.

The tribe is supposed to inter-marry with any Jat tribe.

Being such a small tribe they can give but few men to the Army and civil.

63. Mair and Mair Manhas

1. *Male population.*—7,800. (Census (1931)

2. *Locality.*—The Mairs are found chiefly in the Chakwal tahsil of the Jhelum district and are also scattered about the adjacent of districts Rawalpindi and Attock.

3, *Leading families.*—Their headmen are known as "Choudhri." In Chakwal is the family of an (late) Extra Assistant Commissioner. Other families of standing are in Kot Rupwal Ghugh, Badshahan, Chakral Chak Naurang and Mian Mir.

4, *History and particulars.*—The Mairs say they are Manhas Rajputs (Manhas being a word denoting agricultural pursuits, applied to Rajputs who took to agricultural) and that they are Dogars of the same stock as the Maharaja of Jammu : this has apparently been admitted by one Maharaja.

Their ancestors lived in the hilly country west of Jammu.

The Dhanni country (Chakwal) was then part of Kingdom of the Dogras, and was given to their forefather, Bhagiar Der, as his share of the ancestral estates. He went there with his following, some time before the advent of Babar.

The country was then occupied by wandering Gujjars who were rejected by the Mairs. The eastern part of the Chakwal tahsil was covered by a great lake which Babar drained by cutting through the Ghori Gala by which the Bunha torrent now escapes. The Mairs took up the drained country.

The Mairs like their neighbours, the Kassars, are passionate and revengeful. They gave the Sikhs much trouble, and it required Ranjit Singh's presence in their tract to bring them to order·

Thep joined the Sikhs in 1848 and on making over a lady (Mrs. George Lawrence) to them, all their Jagirs were confiscated by the English.

In the 1857 they distinguished themselves by some services and by good conduct, and thus obtained a reversal of their attainder.

The Mairs inter-marry with the Kassars and, to a less extent, with the Kahuts.

There appears to be a social distinction between the ordinary Mair and Mair Manhas ; the latter consider themselves Rajputs and of the aristocracy of the tribe.

Physically the Mairs are active and well made and are high-spirited; well suited in most respects for military service.

64. Maldial.

1. *Male population.*—57,00 (Census 1931)

2. *Locality.*—The Maldial inhabit both banks of the Mahl river in Poonch (Azad Kashmir).

Particulars.—The tribe claims to be of Moghal descent, but can produce no evidence to substantiate this claim, their neighbours do not allow it and will not give their daughters in marriage to the tribe.

The men are of medium stature and well-built.

65. Maliar.

Maliars are cultivators and gardeners and are the same a Malis or Baghbans. They are found every where, but are most numerous in Rawalpindi, Attock and Jhelum.

Maliars are fond of calling themselves by the name of some tribe higher in the social, as Awan or Janjua.

They are excellent cultivators.

66. Malik

1. *Male population.*—29,000. (Census 1931)

2. *Particulars.*—The Malik is a tribe of lower Rajput status found in Poonch and Jammu.

They describe themselves as having been brought into Poonch by the Emperor Akbar to guard the passes into Kashmir from the Punjab. They sometimes call themselves Malik Manhas. A certain number are employed in the Kashmir Imperial Service Troops.

They do not marry outside the tribe.

67. Mangral.

1. *Male population.*—About 4,500 (Census 1931).

2. *Particulars.*—Mangrals are of good social position and are found chiefly in the Kotli tahsil of the Mirpur. (Azad Kashmir).

A good number is seving in the Army and some Officers of the tribe have been in the Frontier Force.

They are sometimes known as Mangral Gakkhars but appear to have no real connection with the Gakkhars except that they will not give their daughters to any other tribe. The men are small but of good physique, and they are keen on military employment.

68. Manhas.

1. *Male population.*—Approximately 2,500. (Census 1931).

2. *Locality.*—The tribe is found scattered about in small communities in the Sialkot and Rawalpindi districts.

3. *Leading families.*—There are none of any impartance.

4. *History and particulars.*—The word Minhas or Manhas refers to agriculture and denotes that section of the tribe which took to agricultural pursuits. The Jamwal is the royal branch who do not engage in agriculture. The tribe has an illustrious pedigree and claims to be of Solar origin through Ram Chandra of Ajudhya. Their ancestors

are supposed to have settled in Jammu and Kashmir. They now occupy rather a humble place in the Rajput scale of precedence. They nevertheless make excellent soldier.

69. Manj.

1. *Male population.*—About 8,000. (Census 1931).

2. *Locality.*—Pre-partition this tribe belonged mainly to the Jullundur district but is found in Lahore and Rawalpindi.

The Alpials of the Rawalpindi district claim to be Manj Rajputs.

3. *History and particulars.*—The Manj claim to be connected with the Bhatti, and descended from a mythical Raja name Salvahan. South of the Sutlej the Manj Rais of Talwandi and Raikot ruled over a very extensive territory till dispossessed of it by Ranjit Singh and his Sikhs. North of that river the Manj never succeeded in establishing a principality.

With the exception of the Alpial branch, the Manj has now little to recommend him except his good physique. Too proud to till the land themselves they cultivate it as a rule through the agency of servants, or lease it out to tenants. In either case they only receive landlord's profits, while the sturdier Jat, cultivating with his own hands, reaps the profit of both landlord and cultivator.

The conversion of the tribe to Islam probably took place in the reign of Shahab-ud-Din Ghory, *i.e.*, in the middle of the 12th century.

70. Mekan.

1. *Male population.*—Probably 3,000. (Census 1931).

2. *Locality*.—The Mekan are chiefly found in the Shahpur district, and also, in very small numbers, in Jhelum Multan and the Kharian tahsil of Gujrat.

3. *Headmen*.—The best known of the tribe are two families of the Zaildars in the Shahpur tahsil, in the villages Kot Bhai Khan and Kot Pahlwan.

4. *Particulars*.—The Mekan are said to be of Panwar origin, descended from the same ancestor as the Dhudhi. They are a partial tribe and are said to be somewhat turbulent.

They rank as Rajput and are generally of fine physique.

71. Meos or Mawatis

Male population.—71,633. (Census 1931).

The early history and origin of the Meos is abscure; they themselves claim Rajput origin, alleging descent from an ancestor converted in the time of Kut-ub-Din. It seems probable, however, that the Minas and Meos are connected and they are probably both representatives of the earlier non-Ayran inhabitants of the country. In former times the Meos were noted for their turbulance. As soldiers they are cheery and willing workers. Their physique is excellent as they have strong thighs and broad chests. There is ample and good material for enlistment in infantry.

72. Moghal.

1. *Male Population*.—There are over 100,000 so-called Moghals males in the Punjab. (Census 1931).

2. *Locality*.—Moghals are common throughout the Punjab but the census returns show that the Jhelum district

contains the largest number, over 11,000 males in that district having returned themselves as Moghal; Rawalpindi with nearly, 8,000 and Attock with 5,000 come next.

3. *History and particulars.*—Moghuls or Mongols, either entered the country with Babar or were attracted during the reign of his dynasty. Of the figures given above only a small number are of pure Mongolian blood. Irrespective of the mixture of blood resulting from inter-marriage of the Moghals with the local castes, there is a strong tendency among men of low status to claim Moghal descent, and it has even become the fashion of late years for some well-known tribes to describe themselves as Moghal. Among such are the following :—

Ghebas, Kassar, Phaphras, Tanaolis, and even sometime the Gakkhars. In "A History of the Moghals of Central Asia" by N. Elias and E. D. Rose we find the following :—"In origin there is little difference between the Turk and Moghal. The word 'Moghal' even where it is used in an ethnic sense, is frequently misapplied, and so extended at certain periods in history, as to comprise many tribes of real Turki race (among the others) until large numbers of people who were not of Moghal race came to be called Moghals. This habit appears to have been prevalent first in the time of Chingiz Khan and his immediate successors, and subsequently during the ascendency of the Chaghatai (or so called Moghal) dynasty in India. The third conclusion is that the application and signification of all these names.—Turk, Tartar and Moghal—varied at different times and in different countries."

The true Moghal has great pride of race, which feeling usually accompanied those qualities which we look for in the soldier.

The best known clans are—The Barlas, Chaghatta and Kiani, whilst in the Lahore district are some known are Turkmal and Ghori. The true Moghal will always add "Beg" to his name, and generally uses "Mirza" as a prefix.

A man who calls himself Moghal but who cannot tell the name of his clan should generally be rejected as an undesirable.

73 Narma.

The Narma is a Rajput tribe with a male population of 3,300, found chiefly in the Bagh tahsil of Poonch and the Kotlia tahsil of Azad Kashmir. They are also to be found in small numbers in Kahutta, Gujar Khan and Rawalpindi Tahsil.

Their tradition connects them with Puran. said to be a son of Raja Salvahan from whom also come the Bhattis and Manj Rajputs.

They connect themselves with the Solhan Rajput with whom they inter-marry.

They are generally of good physique, short and sturdy with good legs.

74. Naru.

1. *Male population.*—About 12,000. (Census 1931).

2. *Locality.*—Pre-partition this tribe belonged mainly to the Hoshiarpur and Jullundur districts, and a few in Gurdaspur and Amritsar. Now in Pakistan they one found in Lahore and Rawalpindi and Sahiwal and Multan.

4. *Headmen.*—Their headmen were "Ranas" of

the four "Parganas" in Hoshiarpur, and one in Jullundur (India).

5. *History and particulars.*—The Narus say that they are Surajbansi Rajputs converted in the time of Mahmud of Ghazni. They came originally from Muttra and thence through Jaisalmer to the Punjab.

Their ancestor, Raja Tilochand, having applied for help in a civil war to the King of Delhi, was sent to conquer the Punjab, which he did, and in return was made ruler of the country,

His son Nihal Chand, became a Muhammadan, and assumed the name of Naru Shah. Naru Shah first settled at Mau in Jullundur (India) whence his son RatanPal founded Phillaur. Thence were founded the four Naru "parganas" of Hariana, Bajwana, Sham Chaurasi and Ghorewaha in Hoshiarpur and Bahr in Jullundur (India). The chief man in each of these "parganas" is known as "Rai" or "Rana".

75. Panwar.

1. *Male population.*—About 30,000. (Census 1931).

2. *Locality.*—The Panwar is found in the Bahawalpur State, in Multan, Sahiwal and Lahore.

3. *History and particulars.*—The Panwar or Pramara was once the most important of the Agnicula Rajputs. "The world is the Pramaras" is an ancient saying denoting their extensive sway, and the Nankot Marusthali, extending along and below the Sutlej from the Indus almost to the Jamna, signified the Maru Asthal or arid territory occupied by them. But many centuries have passed since

they were driven from their possessions, and in 1826 they held in independent sway only the small State of Dhat in the desert.

Ranghars (Musalman Rajputs).

The Musalman Rajputs of the Ambala Division are commonly known as Ranghars. After partition they have settled down in the Lahore, Sheikhupura and Multan districts.

They belong chiefly to the Batti, Chauhan, Ponwar, Jatu, Taoni and Tonwar clans. They are much superior in quality to the Eastern Rajput.

76 Phaphra or Phiphra

1. *Male population.*—350. As shown in the census returns (1931) but from the number who are serving in the army there must be many more than this.

2. *Locaity.*—The Phaphra have a few villages at the foot of the Salt Range, east of Pind Dadan Khan in the Jhelum district.

3. *Headmen.*—A retired Extra Assistant Commissioner and Subedar Major are perhaps, the most influential members of the tribe.

5. *History and particulars.*—The Phaphras follow the prevailing fashion and call themselves Moghals, to which they have no claim.

The tribe is classed as "semi-Jat" ranking somewhat above the Jat status in popular estimation. They intermarry with the Lillas, Gondals and Varaich, etc., who are for the most part certainly Jats.

In character, customs and physique they do not seem

to differ from the other agricultural tribes of the Jhelum district.

77. Phularwan.

1. *Male population.*—About 1,700. (Census 1931).

2. *Locality.*—The Phularwan occupy a compact block of 10 villages in the Zaffarwal tahsil of Sialkot round Chobara and also few villages in the Phillaura tahsil.

3. *Headmen.*—The Zaildar of Pindi Bago.

4. *History and particulars.*—Little is known about this tribe and it is not mentioned in the census returns.

The "Rivaj-i-am" describes it as Rajput, and accounts for it as follows :—

One Feroze Shah became a convert to Islam and was given land in the Jhang district, where he founded a village called Bharwal. For five generations his descendants lived in Bharwal, they then offended the authorities and all were put to the sword, except one Manga, who escaped. Manga came to Zaffarwal and his descendants established themselves in their present habitations.

Phuler Awan has been suggested as the derivation of the tribal name, but there appears to be nothing definite to support this supposition.

78. Punjabi Pathan.

Male population.—1,93,835. (Census 1931).

The Pathan is generally associated with the Trans-Indus districts, but scattered about the Punjab are to be found small colonies of Pathans who, in order to distinguish them from the Pashtu-speaking Pathan of the borders, are here termed Panjabi Pathans.

These non-frontier Pathans are usually known by the town or locality in which they are settled, *e.g.*, Kasur Pathans, Multani Pathans. These colonies of Pathans are accounted for by Sir Densil Ibbetson in the following manner :—

"During the Lodi and Sur dynasties many Pathans migrated to India especially during the reign of Bahlol Lodi and Sher Shah Suri. These naturally belonged to the Ghilzai section from which those kings sprung.

But large numbers of Pathans accompanied the armies of Mahmud Ghaznavi, Shahab-ud-Din and Babar, and many of them obtained grants of land in the Punjab plains and founded Pathan colonies which still exist. Many more Pathans have been driven out of Afghanistan by internal feuds or by famine and have taken refuge in the plains east of the Indus.

The tribes most commonly to be found in Punjab are the Yusufzai including the Mandahr, the Lodi Kakar, Sarwani, Orakzai, the Karlauri tribes and the Zamand Pathans. Of these the most widely distributed are the Yusufzai, of whom a body of 12,000 accompanied Babar in the final invasion of India, and settled in the plains of India and the Punjab. But as a rule the Pathans who have settled away from the frontier have lost all memory of their tribal divisions, and indeed almost all their national characteristics.

Multani Pathans.—The descendants of Zamand very early migrated in large numbers to Multan, to which province they furnished rulers, till the time of Aurangzeb, when a number of the Abdali tribe under the leadership of Shah Husain were driven from Kandahar by tribal feuds, took refuge in Multan, and being early supplemented by other of their kinsmen who were expelled by Mir Wais, the great Ghilzai chief, conquered Multan and founded the tribe well known in the Punjab as Multani Pathans.

Zahid Khan Abdali was appointed Governor of Multan with the title of Nawab, at the time of Nadir Shah's invasion. Multan was Governed by different members of this family, until in 1818 the city was captured by the Sikhs under Ranjit Singh, after a heroic defence in which the Nawab and five of his sons were slain.

Kasur Pathans.—When the Zamand section was broken up, the Khweshgi clan migrated to the Ghorband defile, and a large number marched thence with Babar and found great favour at his hands and those of Humayun, One section of them settled at Kasur, and are known as "Kasuria Pathans"

The Kasuria Pathans increased in numbers and improtance until the chiefs thought themselves strong enough to refuse to pay tribute to the Moghals. After some severe fighting the Kasuria Pathans were compelled to give in, they never lost heart however and maintained their independence until 1807, when they were finally subdued by the Sikhs. After the confiscation of Kasur by Ranjit Singh, the Pathans were ordered to remain on the left bank of the Sutlej where their leader was assigned the Jagir of Mamdot.

Besides these two better known clans, there are,

as already mentioned others to be found in small colonies throughout the Punjab.

Many distinguished Officers, from cavalry regiments, belong to this class.

79. Rajputs.

The Punjabi Musalman Rajput tribes described in this chapter have been mainly those of the Rawalpindi Civil Division. The term Rajput has to a large degree come to mean a social grade rather than an ethnological term among Punjabi Musalmans. The Census Report of 1931 gives the male population af Punjabi Musalman Rajputs as 9,19,165.

80. Ranjha.

1. *Male population.*—About 8,000, (Census 1931)

2. *Locality.*—The bulk of the Ranjhas are to be found in the Bhera tahsil of the Shahpur district, there are a few also in Gujranwala and Jhelum.

3. *Headmen.*—The most influential members of the tribe are the Zaildars of Mid Ranjha and Bhadar in the Bhera tahsil. The lumbardars of Pind Dadun Khan and Lilla in the Jhelum district are men of some standing.

4.—*History and particulars.*—The Ranjhas are generally classed as Jat though they are Bhatti Rajputs. Latterly a few of the tribe have claimed Koreshi origin. They closly resemble the Gondals, with whom they intermarry.

The Ranjhas show little desire for military service.

81. Sakhal.

This tribe is found chiefly in the Mirpur district where they own a group of villages round Khattar. A few are also in Poonch. They are "Sahu" and claim to be Gakkhars. The Admal Gakkhars describe the Sakhal as having formerly been servants of the Gakkhars.

The tribe is a small one.

82. Salehria.

1 *Male population.*—Between 12,000 and 14,000. (Census 1931).

2. *Locality.*—The Salehria are mostly found in the Zaffarwal (Sialkot) and Shakargarh. There are some also in the Lahore district.

3. *Headmen.*—The best known and most influential family belong to a village named Rupar Chak in the Zaffarwal tahsil, its head is a Zaildar.

4.—*History and particulars.*—The Salehria are Sombansi Rajputs who trace their descent from Raja Saigal, of fabulous antiquity, and from his descendant Chandra Gupta. They say that their ancestors came from the Deccan, as part of a military force, to suppress an insurrection among the Khokkars, and settled in Sialkot.

83. Sarara.

1. *Male population.*—4,600. Census 1931).

2. This tribe is met with only in the Boi tract, between the Thandiani Range and the Kunher river, in the Hazara district.

They connect themselves with both the Dhunds and the Tonaolis, but say at the same time that they come from Pakpattan in the Sahiwal district. The tribe is classed as Sahu and inter-marry on equal trems with the Dhunds.

Their physique is above the average.

84 Satti.

1. *Male population.*—9,730. (Census 1931).

2. *Locality.*—The Satti occupy the lower range of the Murree hills in the Murree and Kahuta tahsils of the Rawalpindi district.

3. *Leading families.*—The head of the Sattis lives at Kamra blow the Narh hill. Another good family is at Chujjana in the Murree tahsil, the head of which is a Zaildar.

4. *History and particulars.*—Next to the Dhunds the Sattis are the largest and most important of the hill tribes of the Rawalpindi district. They occupy the whole of the Kotli spur in the Murree tahsil and they divide the whole of the mountainous portion of the Kahuta tahsil with the Jasgams.

They are probably of the same descent as the Dhunds who pretend to look down on them. They were at one time the traditional enemies of the Dhunds but at the present day the two tribes have no feud and inter-marry freely.

The Sattis have two traditions as to their origin, one connects them with Hazrat Abbas, the paternal of the *prophet* ✢ (peace be upon him) while the other makes them the offspring of one Takht Khan, who came with Timur to Delhi. The Dhunds account for the Sattis in yet another manner which is absolutely rejected by them as false.

There is little doubt that they were originally Hindu, probably Ponwar Rajput's, whose conversion to Islam is of comparatively recent date.

The tribe came to English assistance when the Dhunds attacked Murree in 1857.

Holdings among them are very small and without military service they could not live. The tribe is of good social standing and among them tribal feeling is strong. They hold together and look up to there headman.

They make first-rate soldiers, enlist readily, and are always in great demend.

85. Sayad.

1. *Male population.*—Over 2,50,000. (Census 1931).

2. *Locality.*—Sayads are found everywhere in the Punjab. (West Pakistan).

3. *History and particulars.*—True Sayads are the descendants of Hazrat Ali, Muhammad's son-in-law, who married Fatima *Prophet's* (Be peace up on him) daughter. Many Sayads, however, profess to be his descendants through other wives.

The Sayads of to-day obviously contain a very large mixture of Indian blood, partly by marrying wives from the Indian Muslims of other castes and partly by the tendency of the lower castes to stop gradually into the folds of that holy caste. An immense number of those who profess to be Sayads have really no claim to the title. In the Eastern Punjab they form a comparatively small portion of the population, and are mostly the descendants of true Sayads who followed the Muslim conquerors, and were given grants of land which their descendants continue to enjoy. In the Central and Western Punjab, and more especially on the Frontier, on the Indus, and in the Salt Range, ther are numerous.

As a rule they are cultivators and depend more upon their income from " Piri Muridi," *i. e.*, dues received as holy people, than on agriculture. Their influence on the whole is declining, but they still have considerable power. They are as a rule intelligent. Their social position is very high and they will not give their daughters in marriage to any one except a Sayed or Koreshi, while tribes of the highest social standing marry their daughters to Sayads.

Sayads generally add Shah to their names and are respectfully addressed as " Shahji ". They are found in every branch of the army and opinions differ greatly as to their value as soldiers.

Probable the most compact colony of Sayads are those of the Kagan valley in Hazara, descendants of Jala Baba, who led the Swathi invasion into Hazara. It required an expediton in 1852 to enforce complete sub-mission.

The following are the principal sub-divisions in the Punjab : —

Hasani, Bokhari, Gilani, Hussaini, Mashaidi, Shirazi, Zaidi, Jafiri, Gardazi. Most Sayads are "Pirs," having a large following of "Murids" or disciples.

86. Sheikh.

1. *Male population.*—1,87,370. (Census 1931).

2. *Locality.*—Sheikhs are met with everywhere throughout the Punjab.

3. *Origin and particulars.*—The word Sheikh means "learned," and was originally applied to holy immigrants from Arabia, but it came to be used for converts from Hinduism. A man may be a Sheikh by birth or become one if he is not a Muslim.

The term Sheikh includes over 1,000 sub-castes, many of which appear to have assumed high sounding titles. All Koreshis are Sheikhs but, except in a few localities, they prefer to be known as Koreshis.

87. Sial.

1. *Male population.*—About 50,000. (Census 1931).

2. *Locality.*—The bulk of the Sials are in the Jhang and Multan districts: in the former they are located in Shorkot and Jhang tahsils and the latter in the Kabirwala tashil. They are found also in lesser numbers, in Sahiwal, Shahpur, Muzaffargarh, Dera Ghazi Khan, the Chenab Colony and the Bahawalpur State.

3. *Leading families.*—The descendants of Kabir Khan, the 17th Sial chief, who died in 1801, live in Jhang-Maghiana.

Other families of standing are at Kharanwala, Bad Rajbana and Rustam Sargana. In the Multan district the best known are those of Kund Sargana and Bager.

4. *History and particulars.*—The Sials are descended from Taj Shankar a Ponwar Rajput, whose home was at Daranagar, between Allahabad and Fattehpur. A branch of the Ponwars had previously emigrated from their native country round Delhi to Jaunpur, and it was there that Rai Shankar was born. One story has it that Rai Shankar had three sons—Seu, Teu and Gheu - from whom have descended the Sials of Jhang, the Tiwanas of Shahpur, and the Ghebas of Pindi Gheb. Another tradition states that Sial was the only son of Rai Shankar, and that the ancestors of the Tiwanas and Ghebas were only collateral relations of Shankar and Sial. Owing to dissensions among the members of the family, Sial emigrated during the reign of Ala-ud-din Ghori to the Punjab. Sial in his wanderings came to Pakpattan, and was there converted to the Muslim religion by the eloquent exhortation of the sainted Baba Farid رحمت نه عليه of Pakpattan.

The alleged connection of the Sials with the Tiwanas and Ghebas is most improbable. The tribe is undoubtedly of Rajput origin and migrated west during the reign of Ala-ud-din Ghori when many Rajput families, including the ancestors of the Kharrals, Tiwanas, Ghebas and Chaddars, emigrated from the provinces of Hindustan to the Panjab. Crossing the river Ravi in its lower reaches, the tribe appears to have reached the Chenab in the vicinity of Shorkot in the 14th century, and to have found it necessary to entrench itself against the local tribes, in forts, which mark the country. From this base they appear to have spread north and south along the river, the Thal proving an insuperable barrier to their further progress westward.

The Sials appear to have reached the zenith of their power shortly after Ahmed Shah Abdali's first invasion of the Punjab (1754-55). After a brief period of prosperity, the tribe gradually succumbed to the Sikhs, and was finally conquered by Ranjit Singh, though still retaining considerable political importance.

About one-fifth of the tribes has returned itself as Jat, and the remainder as Rajput.

They appear to have no connection with the town of Sialkot.

88. Sohlan.

The Sohlan is a Rajput tribe connected with the Narma.

The Muslim section is found chiefly in the Mirpur district of Azad Kashmir.

Their physique and characteristics are much the same as the Narma with whom they inter-marry.

The tribe is a small one.

89. Sudhan.

1. *Male population.*—25,300. (Census 1838)

2. *Locality.*—The Sudhanoti tahsil of Poonch is the home of the Sudhans, but they spread also into the Havali, Bagh and Kotli tahsils and a few even are to be

met with across the Jhelum in the Kahuta tahsi of Rawalpindi.

3. *Leading families.*—The Rais of Alisozel in Sudhanoti is perhaps, the most influential man of the tribe.

Other families of good status are at Neriya Chowki and Kirk in the same tahsil.

4. *History and particulars.*—The Sudhans are the most important tribe of Poonch, and of late years an increasing number have been enlisted in the Army.

They claim Pathan origin and say that they are descendants of Ismail who founded Dera Ismail Khan, and also of one Jassi, who was a Pathan.

According to them they first settled near Kotli, in the Murree hills (not the place of the same name in Jammu territory), which was at that time occupied by Brahmans. A tribe known as the Bagar held the opposite bank of the Jhelum and tyrannised over the Brahmans, who called in the Sudhans to their aid. The Sudhans having defeated the Bagars, seized their country and named it Sudhanoti, it was at this time that they took the name of Sudhan, which they had earned as a compliment to their valour from the Brahmans. If all this has any foundation in fact, it must be very ancient history for there is now no trace of the Bagars in Poonch.

The Sudhan varies in physique, and other desirable qualities, with the locality in which he is found. The best are obtained from Sudhanoti, and the nearer they are to the centre of that tahsil the better they are ; here their physique is excellent.

Large numbers of Sudhans take domestic service and are to be met with in Murree, Rawalpindi and the Galis.

The Sudhans have pride of race and look on themselves as superior to any of the other tribes of Poonch, but they cannot be considerd high class Rajputs, which term, notwithstanding their claim to Pathan origin, they apply to themselves.

They marry chiefly among themselves but also take and give wives to the Maldials and some of the Murree hill tribes.

90. Tarar.

1. *Population.*—11,100. (Census 1931)

2. *Locality.*—They bulk of the Tarars are in the Phallian tahsil of the Gujrat district, the tribe is also met with in Gujranwal, Shahpur, Jhelum and Sialkot.

3. *History and particulars.*—The Tarar rank as Jat though they claim Solar Rajput origin, apparently from Bhatti of Bhatner. They say that their ancestor Tarar took service with Mahmud of Ghazni but that his son Lodhi, from whom they are descended moved from Bhatner to Gujrat, Gujranwala and Shahpur.

They inter-marry with the Gondal, Varaich, Gil, Virk and other leading Jat tribes of the neighbourhood.

91. Tezal.

1. *Population.* About 5,400, (Census 1931)

Locality.—The Tezal are found on the right bank of the Mahl river in the Bagh tahsil of Poonch.

3. *Particulars.*—The tribe appears to be a sub-division of the Kakkhe and ranks as Rajput.

They inter-marry with the Sudhan and Chandal of the same locality.

They are of the short stature but robust physique.

92. Thatal

1. *Population.*—1,276. (Census 1931)

2. *Locality.*—The Shahpur and Jhelum district.

3. *Particulars.*—An obscure tribe of Jat status.

93. Tiwana

1. *Male Population.*—About 1,100. (Census 1931)

2. *Locality.*—Tiwanas inhabit the Thal country west of Kushab in the Shahpur district, a few are also to be found in the Bhera and Shahpur tahsils.

3. *Leading families.*—The Tiwanas although numerically a small tribe possess more families of distinction then any other tribe. In fact, "Maliks" appear to predominate over the ordinary rank and file of the tribe.

The Mitha Tiwana family is by far the most important in the Shahpur district. Its history is given in "The Punjab Chiefs." There are many branches of this family, the wealthiest and probably the most important being that of which Malik Umar Hayat Khan was the head.

Other families of high status are in Hamoka and Hadali.

5. *History and Particulars.*—Notwithstanding their claims to high Hindu Descent, the Tiwanas were until about a century ago an ordinary Punjab Musalman tribe, inhabiting a few villages at the north of the Thal desert. After a severe struggle with their neighbours, the Awans, the head of the clan established independent authority over the Thal, and even after the Sikhs under Ranjit Singh, brought them under subjection, they found it advisable to employ the Tiwana Chiefs as their local Governors. Their earlierhistory represents them as being Ponwar Rajputs who emigrated from Hindustan to the Punjab, probably in 15th century. Their first settlement appears to have been at Jahangir on the Indus, where they became converts to Islam.

Moving eastwards they eventually occupied Shahpur, and in 1680 built Mitha Tiwana.

The Tiwana, rendered valuable service in 1848 when the Multanis rose against English and again in 1857, when they proved their loyalty to the English by furnishing over 1,000 horsemen for the irregular cavalry raised in the Punjab by Lord Lawrence.

The Tiwanas are essentially cavalry soldiers, and also serve in infantry.

Their Maliks breed excellent horses.

Closely related to the Tiwanas are a family of Nums (Bhatti Rajputs) with whom the Tiwanas inter-marry.

94. Traggar.

1. *Population.*—900. (Census 1931)

2. *Locality.*—The Traggar are found only in the Multan and Muzaffar-garh districts.

3. *Particulars.*—This tribe claim to be Bhatti Rajputs, and take their name from their ancestral home at Traggar in Bikanir.

The social position of the tribe is good, they are fond of horses and are anxious to serve in cavalry.

95. Varaich.

1. *Male population.*—About 40,000. (Census 1931)

2. *Locality.*—The Varachi are chiefly found in the Phalia and Gujrat tahsils of the Gujrat district, they have also spread in to Gujranwala Sialkot, Jhelum, Lahore and Rawalpindi.

3. *Leading families.*—The Wazirbad family is the most important and is mentioned in the "Punjab Chief's." At Jallalpur Jattan, in the Gujrat tahsil, there is another family of good status, the head of which is a Zaildar.

4. *History and particulars.*—The Varaich is one of the most important of the Jat tribes of the Punjab. There are many stories as to its origin, the most generally accepted of which is that their ancestor Dhudi was a Jat who came into India with Mahmud of Ghazni and settled in Gujrat. The other stories make them Rajputs, which but few Varaiches claim to be. There is little doubt that Gujrat was their first home and that their movement has been eastwards.

It is a disgrace for a member of the tribe to marry a low caste woman. Their social standing is good, and they marry with the best local tribes.

The conversion of the Varachi to Islam took place comparatively recently.

The physique of the men is excellent and they make good soldiers.

96. Virk

1. *Population.*—16,290. (Census 1931)

2. *Locality.*—The Headquarters of the Virk Musalman's appears to be the Gujranwala and Lahore districts. The tribe is also found in Gujrat, Shahpur, Jhang and Multan.

3. *History and Particulars.*—The Virk claim origin from a Manhas Rajputs named Virak, who left Jammu and settled in Amritsar. They are now of Jat status and they marry freely with Jat tribes of their neighbourhood.

Virks are more Sikhs than Muslims.

The tribe rose to some political importance about the end of the 18th century, when they ruled a considerable tract in Gujranwala and Lahore until subdued by Ranjit Singh.

97. Wattu.

1. *Population.*—24,500. (Census 1931)

2. *Locality.*—The Wattu are to be found along both bank of the Sutlej and Ravi in the Sahiwal and Lyallpur districts. There are some also in the Lahore and Sheikhupura districts.

3. *History and particulars.*—The Wattu are a Bhatti

clan, descended from Rajpal, grandson of the Bhatti Raja Salvahan of Sialkot.

The Sutlej Wattus have now taken to agriculture, and are peaceful and industrious cultivators.

The tribe was coverted to Islam by Baba Farid of Pakpattan in the 13th century.

Wattu's are also good soldiers.

Beside the Punjabi Musalman tribes described in the foregoing pages, there are a large number which are classed in the census returns as Rajput and Jat.

CHAPTER VI.

A brief account of Cis-Indus Pathans, and tribes peculiar to Hazara District N-W-F-P and akin to Pathans.

The Awans and Gujars of Hazara District numbering approximately 50,000 and 70,000 males respectively are spread all over the District, and from long residence therein have acquired the manners, customs. etc. of the Hazara tribes among whom they dwell, are indistinguishable from them and are different to the Awans and Gujars of the Punjab.

Other purely Punjabi Musalman tribes such as Gakhars, Dhunds, Kethwals, Karrals, and Sararas are found in the Southern and South Eastern hills of Hazara District, extend into Rawalpindi and Murre Tehsils. A history of these tribes and also of the Awans and Gujars is given in Chapter V.

Akazais.

1. *Population.*—Muster 1,000 fighting men, (Census 1931)

2. *Locality.*—The left bank of the Indus to the Black Mountain.

3. *History and particulars.*—The Akazais are a tribe of Isazai Yusafzais, they are divided into four clans—the Barat Khel, Aziz Khel, Tasan and Painda Khel.

They should make satisfactory soldiers for the country.

Chagarzais.

Population.—Cis-Indus Chagarzais muster about 2,500 fighting men. (Census 1931)

Locality.—Both banks of the Indus from the Trans-Indus Dama mountain on the West, to the Black Mountain on Hazara Border.

History and particulars.—The Chagarzai are a tribe of Malizai Yusafzais, closely allied by family to the Bunerwals. They are divided into three clans, the Firoz Khel entirely Trans-Indus and the Nasrat Khel and Basi Khel on both banks of the Indus.

The Chagarzais are a purely race owning cows, buffaloes and goats. They are men of excellent physique, good mountaineers, have a great reputation for bravery and make excellent soldiers for the country.

Chachh Pathans.

1. *Male population.*—About 10,000. (Census 1931)

2. *Locality.*—The Chachh plain in the northern portion of Attock Tehsil, Attock District, on the left bank of the Indus.

History and particulars.—Many Pathans have migrated from Afghanistan, Tribal Territory and Trans-Indus Territory for various causes during the past two centuries and taken refuge in the plains to the East of the Indus. The Pathans in the Chachh area have retained their coustoms and language and are mainly decendants of the Yusafzai including the Mandaur, the Lodi, the Tarin and the Dilazak tribes.

Enterprise is a very marked characteristic of the Chachh Pathan, as an agriculturist he is excellent—he is a curious blend of farmer, trader and is of very good physique, and makes a very good soldier when he does.

Dilazaks.

1. *Male population.*—About 1,200. (Census 1931)

2. *Locality.*—In Haripur Tehsil of Hazara and the Chachh plain of Attock Tehsil.

3. *History and particulars.*—The origin of this tribe is doubtful, they are acknowledged by Pathans as belonging to the Kodai Karlani branch of the Ghurghusht Pathans, but are probably a race of Scythic descent. The formerly occupied the country about Peshawar and the Indus, and on the borders of Ningrahar. They were driven across the Indus by the Yusafzais, Muhammadzais, Mohmands, and Khalils, at a last fight near Kapur-da Garhi in the Yusafzai plain, in the 16th century.

They make satisfactory soldiers for the country.

Hasanzais.

1. *Population.*—Cis-Indus Hasanzais muster about 1,000 fighting men (census 1931)

2. *Locality.*—Both banks of the Indus, the Cis-Indus portion living on the Black Mountain and the Trans-Indus portion immediately opposite them.

3. *History and particulars.*—The Hasanzais are a tribe of Isazai Yusafzais. The tribe is divided into 11 clans, six living Cis-Indus and 5 Trans-Indus. The Khan Khel

is considered the Chief clan and from it is elected the Khan of the Isazais, otherwise known as the Sahib-e-Dastar (master of the Turban.)

Dis-Indus—

1. Nasrat Khel.
2. Mamu Khel.
3. Dada Khel.
4. Mir Ahmad Khel.
5. Sayads.
6. Khan Khel.

Trans-Indus—

1. Lukman Khel.
2. Nanu Khel.
3. Zakaria Khel.
4. Kotwal.
5. Isa Khel.

They should make satisfactory soldiers for the country.

Jaduns.

1. *Male population.*—In Hazara 6,500. (Census 1931)

2. *Locality.*—Abbottabad and Haripur Tehsils of the Hazara District,

3. *Chief families.*—The Hassazai family of Dhamtour once held the Khanship of the tribe and are still looked up to. Other families hold jagirs of Banda Pir Khan and Bandi.

History and particulars.—The Jaduns are an offshoot of the Transfrontier Jaduns of the Mahaban Range. About the end of the 17th century, they crossed the Indus and spread up the Dor Valley as high as Abbottabad, latter they further extended their holdings at the expense of the Dilazaks and the Karrals. At the present day their settlements are along the banks of the Dor between Bagra and Mangal, part of the Abbottabad plateau and its neighbourhood, and in the Nillan Valley.

The divisions of the tribe are :

1. *Solar—*
   - (*i*) Mat Khwazai.
   - (*ii*) Utazai.
   - (*iii*) Sulimanzai.

2. *Mansur—*
   - (*i*) Daulatzai.
   - (*ii*) Musazai.
   - (*iii*) Khadarzai.

3. *Hassazai.*

The men are of good physique but small stature, they make good soldiers for the country.

Khattaks.

A very complete description of Khattaks is given in the Hand book on Pathans. The following sections of this tribe are found in the Punjab :

Part of the Saghris, inhabiting the left bank of the Indus about Makhad in the south Western portion of Pindigheb Tehsil of Attock District. The Bhangi Khel, inhabiting the Mountainous tract north of Kalabagh in the Isa Khel Tehsil of Mianwali District.

Mishwani

1. *Male population.—*3,000. (Census 1931)

2. *Locailty.*—The north Eastern end of the Gandghar Range in the Haripur Tehsil of Hazara.

3. *Chief families.*—There are several Maliks of good standing, they are all in or near Srikot, their chief village.

4. *History and particulars.*—The Mishwanis are Ghurghusht Pathans, said to be descended from a Sayad, Muhammad-i-Gisu Darez, by a Shirani woman and thus Allied to the Shiranis, Ushtaranas, and Gandapurs. Their original home was probably in Baluchistan whence they attacked themselves as retainers to the Yusafzais in their return to the Peshawar Valley in the 15th or 16th century. A portion of them accompanied the Utmanzai Yusafzais into the Hazara District.

They are a sturdy industrious and well behaved race and their loyalty and courage are beyond question. Major Abbott found in them his staunchest supporters in 1848 and described them as "one of the bravest races in the world." The chief clans are :—

1. Mani Khel.
2. Hasain Khel.
3. Dura Khel.

Niazis.

1. *Male population*—

Mianwali	19,500
Kohat	2,500
Bannu	2,000
Dehra Ismail Khan	500
	24,500

(Census 1931)

2. *Locality.*—On both banks of the Indus chiefly in the Isa Khel and Mianwali Tehsils of the Mianwali District.

3. *History and particulars.*—The Niazis are a Pathan tribe descended from Niazai one of the three sons of Ibrahim, surnamed Lodai. They are thus Lodi Pathans and akin to the Dotanni, Prangis, Surs, etc. After their defeat by the Marwats at the beginning of the 16th century, they found a home in the Trans-Indus portion of the Mianwali District, east of the Tanga Darra by expeling or reducing to serfdom the Awans and Jats who they found there. The Sarhang section subsepuently occupied the left bank of the Indus. They are still fairly numerous in Kohat and Bannu Districts and are found in small numbers in Dera Ismail Khan. Part of the tribe is nomadic, trading between Khorasan and the Derajat, pitching their camp at Isa Khel in the winter. Although their language (Pashto) has been completely replaced by Punjabi in the Mianwali Tehsil and is undergoing the same process in the Isa Khel Tehsil, they retain great pride in being Pathans. The Awans and Jats living amongst them from the great mass of the population but are in the great majority of cases only tenants. The tribe is almost entirely agricultural, they have been enlisted for the Infantry and prove a great success as soldiers, their physique is very much above the average.

Swatis.

1. *Male population.*—20,000 (Census 1931).

2. *Locality.*—The Swatis called the Swatis of Pakhli inhabit Konsh, Bhogarmang, the Chatar Plain, Part of

Agor and some villages on the Kamhar River in the Kagan Vally, all in Hazara District.

The Swatis of Allai, in independent Territory, extend northwards from Mansehra Tehsil to Kohistan.

3. *History and particulars.*—The Swatis claim to be Pathans, descendants of the people who inhabited Swat and Buner before the Yusafzai invasion which drive them into Hazara about the end of the 17th century.

The are divided into the following clans :—

1. Jehangirai.
2. Argoshal Mulkal.
3. Ishmaili.
4. Mir Khani Sulemani.
5. Sarkheli.
6. Mandrawi.
7. Panjghol. { Shamota. / Lochal.
8. Doodhyal { Mayor. / Bishgrami.
9. Panjmiral.
10. Alisheri.

These Divisions are represented by a number of chiefs, namely, those of :—

Ghari Habibullah.
Mansehra.
Giddarpur.
Doodhyal.
Bhogarmang.
Batal.
Batigram.
Dhannial.

The country is rich in cultivation and cattle and the population is dense. There are a number of large and thriving villages.

Tanaolis.

1. *Male population.*—35,000, of whom 20,000 are feudal Tanawal.

2. *Locality.*—The Hindwal section occupy feudal or upper Tanawal and extend to the right bank of the Indus, the Pallal lower Tanawal, including Badhnak and a number of villages in the Garhian tract of the Mansehra Tehsil.

3. *Leading families.*—The recognised Chief is the Nawab of Amb (feudal Tanawal).

The leading clan of the Pallals is the Labhya, commonly called Suba Khani, whose best known families are those of Phuhar, Bir and Shingri which are represented by three Jagirdars—besides these there are the Jagirs of Sherwan and Chamhad.

4. *History and particulars.*—The Tanaolis claim descent from Amir Khan, a Barlas Moghal, whose two sons Hind Khan and Pal Khan crossed the Indus about the end of the 17th century, from the country round Mahaban, and settled in the Mountainous area now held by them and named after the tribe—Tanawal.

The Tanaolis are industrious cultivators of good Physique make very good soldiers. Punjabi is the Mother Tongue though a few speak Pushtu as well, they have many Pathan customs and take much pride in their dress and appearance.

The sub-divisions of the tribe are :—

1. *Hindwal.—*

   (*i*) Jamal ⎰ Charyal.
   ⎨ Ledhyal.
   ⎱ Abdwal.

   (*ii*) Saryal. ⎰ Lalal.
   ⎨ Hedral.
   ⎱ Baizal.

   (*iii*) Jalwal.

   (*iv*) Bohal.

   (*v*) Baigal.

   (*vi*) Tekral.

   (*vii*) Ansal.

   (*viii*) Masand.

   (*ix*) Rains.

2. *Pallal.*

   (*i*) Labhya (Suba Khani).

   (*ii*) Matyal.

   (*iii*) Bainkaryal.

   (*iv*) Dairal.

   (*v*) Sadhal.

   (*vi*) Judhal.

   (*vii*) Baigal.

   (*viii*) Tekral.

   (*ix*) Asnal.

   (*x*) Masand.

   (*xi*) Rains.

3. *Bhujal.—*

Tarins

1. *Male population—*1,000 (Census 1931).

2. *Locality.—*Hazara District and Attock Tahsil.

3. *History and particulars.—*The Tarins are Sarbani Pathans, descendants of Tarin, son of Sharkaban, son of Sarban. According to tradition Tarin had three sons Abdul Khan, Tor Khan and Spin Khan—from the first are descended the Saddozais and Durranis; from the second and third the Tarins themselves. Some Tor Tarins lie in the Haripur Plain and there are a few Spin Tarin in Tarbela and Attock tahsil, the remainder of the tribe are to be found in the Quetta Peshin District. The Tarins came to Hazara with the Utmanzai Yusafzais early in the 18th century and rose to be the most important tribe in Lower Hazara, but with the advent of the Sikhs their power waned.

The Tarin are divided into the following clans.

Tor Tarins—

1. Saigi.
2. Nurzai.
3. Makhiani.
4. Malikyar,
6. Alizai.
6. Abubakar.

Spin Tarins—

1. Zaam.
2. Wanechi.

3. Semani.
4. Raisani.
5. Marpani.
6. Lasiani.
7. Adwani.
8. Malgrani.

The men are of good physique and make good soldiers for the country.

Tarkhelis.

1. *Male population.*—500. (Census 1931).

2. *Locality.*—The Khari tract and the lower end of the Gandgarh range in Hazara, with several villages in the Attock Tehsil.

3. *History and particulars.*—The Tarkhelis are a sub-section of the Alazai Utmanzais, they do not inter-marry with the rest of Utmanzai, and their customs also differ. Inheritance is *per capita* and not by the *chundawand* rule. The Tarkheli make excellent soldiers.

Turks.

1. *Male population.*—About 2,000 (Census 1931).

2. *Locality.*— Haripur and Mansehra Tehsil of Hazara District.

3. *Chief families.*—The Jagirdars of Biali in the Mansehra Tehsil is probably the best known and most influential man of the tribe in Hazara District.

4. *History and particulars.*—The name of Turk is a Tartar word meaning "Wanderer". The Turks are

descendants of the Mogolian Karlagh Turks who entered India with Tamerlane in 1399 A. D. at one time they dominated Hazara District, but gradaully Pathan and other tribes evicted them from their possessions and in A. D. 1786 they appealed to Timur Shah Durani to reinstate them in Manakrai—the Headquarters of the clan near Haripur, from which the Gurgust Pathans had ousted them.

They are now of little importance, but make satisfactory soldiers.

Utmanzai.

1. *Male population*—2,600. (Census 1931).

2. *Locality.*—Both banks of the Indus, the branch on the right bank is independent, musters about 400 fighting men, and is situated on a narrow strip between Gadun country and the Indus—their chief villages are Kabal and Kaya : the branch on the left bank inhabits the Tarbela—Khalsa tracts in Hazara on both banks of the Siran, from above its junction with the Dor River to the Indus.

3. *History and particulars.*—The Utmaazais are a tribe of a Mandanr Yusufzais, the physique of the Cis-Indus branch is good and they make excellent soldiers. Tarbela is a Kanazai centre and is the principal village.

The are divided into the following clans :—

1. Alazai, Tarkhe lis.
2. Kanazai.
3. Akazai.
4. Saddozai—(Trans-Indus).
   - 1. Aba Khel.
   - 2. Mir Ahmad Khel.
   - 3. Umar Khel
   - 4. Bazid Khel.

Lightning Source UK Ltd.
Milton Keynes UK
UKHW042239090820
367908UK00001BB/166